NØKKEN

A Garden for Children

A Danish Approach to Waldorf-Based Child Care

Helle Heckmann
Translated by Lone Schmidt

SECOND EDITION

Includes selections from A Garden for Kids,
the 2003 celebration of Nøkken

With special thanks to Lone Schmidt for the English translation.

Nøkken was first published in Danish by Forlaget Pimpegrynden under the title *Nøkken — en have for børn*, and in German by the International Association of Waldorf Kindergartens under the title *Nøkken — ein Garten für Kinder im Alter von ein bis sieben Jahren*.

The first English edition was published by the Center for Anthroposophy and the Waldorf Early Childhood Association of North America in 1998.

The booklet *A Garden for Kids* was originally published by Nøkken in 2003 and printed and distributed by WECAN.

Orignal design by Salwen Studios, Keene, NH
Adapted by Lory Widmer

© 2015 Waldorf Early Childhood Association of North America
Second English Edition

Published in the United States
by the Waldorf Early Childhood Association of North America
285 Hungry Hollow Road
Spring Valley, NY 10977
845-352-1690
info@waldorfearlychildhood.org
www.waldorfearlychildhood.org

ISBN: 978-1-936849-30-7

All rights reserved. No part of this book may be reproduced in any form without the written permission of the publisher, except for brief quotations embodied in critical reviews and articles.

CONTENTS

NØKKEN: A GARDEN FOR CHILDREN (1998)
Foreword to the Second Edition by Trisha Lambert • 5
Preface by Helle Heckmann • 7
Introduction by Joan Almon • 11

CHAPTER 1: The Child's Physical Development in the First Year • 17

The Right to Cry • 17

What Environment Do We Wish to Offer the Infant? • 19

The Development of Motor Skills in the First Year • 20

First Quarter • 20

Second Quarter • 21

Third Quarter • 22

Fourth Quarter • 22

Sitting • 23

Pulling Up to Stand • 24

Standing Alone • 25

Walking Alone • 26

CHAPTER 2: The Child-Care Center Nøkken and Its Environment • 27

Staff Relations • 31

Number of Children • 32

Daily Rhythm: Inhaling/Exhaling • 33

A Day in the Life . . . • 37

Parent Relations • 64

Seasonal Celebrations • 64

Birthdays • 66

International Relations • 70

Funding • 72

Afterword by Helle Heckmann • 76

Helle Heckmann—A Short Biography • 77

FROM A GARDEN FOR KIDS: A CELEBRATION OF NØKKEN (2003)

Can I Take Care of Other People's Children? • 78

One Week in the Life of Nøkken • 83

Working with the Will • 91

What I Remember from My Time at Nøkken • 93

The Course of Life • 94

Our Step into Nøkken • 98

"Graduation" Speech • 100

Oh, it's so good to be here! • 101

An Interview with Helle Heckmann • 102

The Power of Imagination • 108

To Be the Mother of a Child in Nøkken • 111

Bibliography • 113

Further Resources • 115

Foreword

It is very exciting to me that this book is being reprinted in a new, expanded edition. *Nøkken* was first published at a time when many people were exploring the meaning of anthroposophical care for the young child. For many reasons more children than ever needed to be cared for outside of their families, and here in North America, early childhood educators were exploring the possibilities of full-time center-based care. This book quickly became an important resource for caregivers considering the important work of caring for young children outside of their own home.

Helle offered us glimpses into the daily life at Nøkken. The slow, easy rhythm of life, one day following another, was simple, yet full. The attention and care that each small child could receive in the context of a larger group gave a beautiful and loving picture of the care given at Nøkken. Proper preparation and planning behind the scenes by the adults, can make for a seamless day with the the children.

For many people, it was a surprise to learn just how much of the day could be spent outside, in nature. Now modern research has shown us just how important and necessary time outdoors for the young child is. The pictures of the youngest children napping in the fresh open air reminded us of the simplicity of old ways but also how healthy such a simple act could be.

Nøkken

Helle is also very good at reminding us that this what is offered at Nøkken; it is not a cookie cutter program that can be transported anywhere, but it is what fits and serves in its own location. This is an very important idea, differing from many mainstream packaged curriculum that are offered today.

Care of the caregiver, another new concept, is included in the book. The role of the caregiver herself is shown to be important, and each caregiver has her own strengths to bring. The inner life of the caregiver is also brought forward as a tool of self-awareness and personal growth that supports the teacher and her work.

As a caregiver of young children myself, this book is a constant source of ideas and inspiration and I refer to it often. I am so grateful that Helle has taken the time and energy to share this glimpse of the program at Nøkken with us. I have shared this book with many people interested in starting on this path of caring for the children of others. It is a fulfilling task, and this book surely is a helpful guide to be savored and enjoyed. In this new edition, which includes further insights from the 2003 booklet *A Garden for Kids* along with beautiful new photographs, I hope it will continue to inspire and enrich us all in our journey with young children.

Trisha Lambert
Davis, California
2015

Preface

This book was inspired by the wish to share my experiences of working with very young children in day care outside their homes. It is an area of child care which still poses many questions, and their solutions are evolving in relationship to human, cultural and physical surroundings.

In my work with young children I came across the work of Dr. Emmi Pikler, who worked in a children's home in Hungary. Through her observation of children, she was able to show the importance of confidence and self-reliance as well as the belief in "being able to," as fundamental to the child's development into a confident adult. By reinforcing the child's confidence in her physical capabilities, and by respecting each child's individual developmental path, we as caregivers and educators can meet the needs of the young child. Emmi Pikler has given me the courage to work with children in a respectful way.

Care of the young child outside the home is a reality in Denmark. It has indeed been the case for the last twenty-five years. A great deal of experience within many pedagogical ideologies has been gained during this time. It seems to me that initiatives in which the young child's spiritual and physical development are central are distinctly lacking. Often economic considerations are the decisive factor. This is not to say that economics is not an important consideration; it just isn't the most important one. Society depends on our children developing into well-functioning adults. If we do not set our most precious resource highest, we are guilty of treachery against humanity.

Following the introduction by Joan Almon, then chairperson of the Waldorf Early Childhood Association of North America, I have described the child's first years of development. The reason for this is that everyone's life in later years is dependent on his opportunity to develop physically at a pace and in the order necessary for him to take hold of his physical body. The attainment of physical equilibrium is dependent on the care giver allowing the child to work on himself in peace and quiet. Since this demands special conditions, we have, at Nøkken, chosen not to have children come before they can walk, since this early stage presents challenges we cannot meet. We have had to make a choice, which means we cannot offer day care which caters to all needs. These limitations mean we cannot satisfy all families' needs. This is not to say that it isn't possible to set up other kinds of day care. In the situation that we have, with its physical, economic, and cultural conditions, we have decided what we can offer. We feel that we are able to give children the opportunity for imitation to the greatest extent to which we are capable. There follows a description of Nøkken's daily routine, how it is built up, and why we do what we do.

It is intended that this book is seen as one possible way to set up a daily life with children. It has been born of the conditions which we have and of the people we are. But the possibilities are endless, as are the children. The important point is that the adult (the teacher) knows why she does what she does, that she works consciously.

I would like to thank Ruth Lassen for the help and support she has given me. Thank you to Jan Christiansen for introducing me to the world of computers. Jan was always there when this manuscript had disappeared into the strangest places in the depths of the computer.

Thank you, too, to the "International committee for the care of young children outside the home," an outgrowth of the International Waldorf Kindergarten Association. Despite difficult working conditions, we meet steadfastly in an atmosphere of optimism and earnestness.

Last but not least, thank you to my three children, Liv, Ege, and Bue, without whom the love in me would never had had the chance to blossom so richly.

Nøkken

Considerations

How can we take care of other people's children? This question remains unresolved. It is the question that inspired the beginning of my work with young children and the one I am still asking. Children are a very delicate subject, a subject where all our feelings are involved. What one parent thinks is right, another feels is wrong. I think it is important that a child's daily life isn't filled with too many "seems," "ought tos," and desires. How can I create a framework for the young child in which the child feels safe, where daily life is predictable, without surprises born of the mood I am in on any particular day? This, of course, doesn't exclude the individuality which every day has.

Helle Heckmann

Copenhagen, Denmark

1998

Introduction

There was once a time when most children were raised in their homes, around the warmth of the hearth. It seems long ago, although here and there it still happens, and there is a growing interest in helping mothers stay at home to raise their children, although the conditions for child rearing are very different than they were a century ago.

In those earlier days, children were generally raised by their mothers with help from grandparents, aunts, and neighbors. The reality of the saying, "It takes a village to raise a child," was known to every family, although often the village was in the form of extended family or urban neighborhood.

This does not mean that there were no problems. As today, there were challenges of alcoholism, abuse, and dysfunction. In addition, mothers often died in childbirth, and children suffered and frequently died from contagious diseases. But whatever the circumstances — healthy or unhealthy — the child generally was brought up in the home by mothers who drew on generations of wisdom about child raising.

For today's children in modern, technologically advanced countries, the situation is radically different. In the United States in 1998, the majority of children under six spend long hours with child-care providers, whether with au pairs in the home, a child-care mother in her own home, or with care providers in a

Nøkken

larger center. Child care often begins at six weeks of age.

Children in child care from infancy on may experience five or six main care givers by the time they go to first grade. Such children are not only away from their own families for long periods of time each day, but lack the consistency of care that promotes attachment and bonding. It is easy to imagine a shallowness of relationship developing just when the child needs examples of depth and commitment, faithfulness, and love.

This is the general picture of child care today, although there are notable exceptions where it is done very well. Current evaluations of child care in the United States indicate that about 10% of child-care centers are considered quite good. About 45% are considered acceptable, and the other 45% are below standard.

Against such a picture of child care, Helle Heckmann's center, Nøkken, stands out in a number of positive ways. Helle accepts children at age one, or when they can walk, and keeps them with her until they are ready for first grade at age seven. Siblings remain together, and the whole group, 25 to 30 strong, functions like a large healthy family, albeit one of unusually large proportions. Children are not divided by age except to meet the nap needs of the younger ones, so they have a chance to be together each day like brothers and sisters. There is also much constancy of staff, for although there is some turnover, Helle and one or two others have remained with the children over many years.

A few things are surprising and may not be directly transferable to other

Introduction

cultures. I think especially of Helle's schedule, which has the children outside for most of their six-hour day with her. This would be considered excessive in many countries, yet it works well for Helle and her children. There is a tradition in Denmark of "forest kindergartens," where city children travel to the woods each day for a kindergarten without walls. There is also a tradition of letting little children nap outside, well wrapped up in layers of wool and secured in sturdy prams, even in wet and wild weather. Such a practice would probably not be well received in some countries, but it works well in Denmark where, it seems to me, the spirit of the Vikings lives on. There are many other practices, however, that can be directly transferred into other cultures.

On the day I visited, I was struck by how healthy and relaxed the children were and wondered how to accomplish the same for the pale, thin children I so often saw in North America. It was clear that in addition to the bracing air and outdoor life, they were also surrounded by human warmth and adults who set a living example of how to nurture and care for the young. An impression which stays strongly with me is of a group of six-year-old girls who were wheeling prams around the garden. Their gestures were so motherly, so loving and caring, that I was certain there must be real babies in the prams. A discreet peek revealed baby dolls. I was moved, for I know how rarely one sees such loving doll play today, in part because children have too few examples of parents taking time to nurture young children day in and day out.

Nøkken

Prior to my visit, I had been very concerned that those raised in child-care centers would have a hard time nurturing their own children when they grew up. Within most child-care centers, children are stratified by age, so a three-year-old does not see an infant being cared for. There is little opportunity to learn about such things through imitation. That Nøkken was able to overcome this problem made a deep impression on me.

In addition, I see how young parents in the United States feel lost over the simplest acts of nurture, such as changing the clothes of their babies. A friend told me that many of the mothers in the parent and infant group she belonged to reported that their little children did not like to have their clothes changed and would cry a great deal on the changing table, especially at night when they were tired. The parents' solution: change the diaper and put the child to bed in the day-time clothes. In some cases, the clothes were left on for two or three days to avoid scenes on the changing table. In contrast, what I observed in Nøkken and similar Waldorf centers is that the changing of clothes is done in such a warm and unhurried manner that it becomes a beloved part of the day for the children and adults, too.

As I watched the children at Nøkken play being mothers, I was struck by the thought that where it was once a village that raised a child, more and more there now need to be such life-filled centers to provide the nurture children need. One great challenge in creating such centers is finding a way to maintain

Introduction

the warmth and commitment of individuals when the hours grow longer than those at Nøkken, which ends its day at 2:30. In the United States and elsewhere, children usually need care until five or six pm, and this places a much greater strain on the teachers and the children.

A number of Waldorf early-childhood teachers in the United States and elsewhere are exploring ways to meet these needs of children. An imaginative picture is developing of a multi-age center that includes mixed age groups from infancy to age six, as well as children up to age twelve who come for care before and after school. It's possible also to develop activities for adolescents, to include the elderly as foster grandparents, or to offer courses for the elderly, for pregnant parents, and more. In such life centers, young children can feel embedded as they once did in their own homes that were part of an extended family or village. It is hoped that within a few years, a number of such centers will exist. There is a growing commitment for such work within the Waldorf early-childhood movement, which now numbers over 1200 programs in fifty countries.

Nøkken is an example of what a healthy center can do for children and families. Its existence has already inspired many care givers, and we hope that this English edition of Helle's book will inspire even more.

For up-to-date information on Waldorf early-childhood programs and child-care centers in English speaking countries, you may contact one of the Waldorf early-childhood associations listed at the back of the book. Meanwhile,

Nøkken

whether you are a parent, a care giver, an early-childhood teacher or adult who cares about children, we feel confidant that you will find much in this book to warm your own heart and lift your spirits.

That this book appears in English is due to the efforts of Helle Heckmann, who arranged for its English translation, and to Susan Weber of the Center for Anthroposophy, who oversaw its production. We are very grateful to them for undertaking this. Sales of the book help to support Nøkken and its related endeavors.

Joan Almon

Chair, Waldorf Early Childhood Association of North America

March, 1998

CHAPTER 1

The Child's Physical Development in the First Year

The Right to Cry

A crying baby can make most people desperate. In our "happy" society, crying equals unhappiness. Now think of a newborn baby, who has few other means of communication during the first five to eight weeks. If you regard crying as a form of communication, your reaction changes. If the baby attracts attention every time she cries, it is not hard to imagine that she will quickly grow dependent on attention.

In the womb, there is no hunger, the temperature is constant, the child is surrounded by darkness with only familiar sounds like the heartbeat; the mother takes care of the breathing. At birth, which is a struggle for life and death, the infant must learn to breathe, experience pressure, feel hunger, go from darkness to light. Only sleep restores the infant to a familiar state. That is why an infant must cry a lot and sleep a lot.

Nøkken

There is no doubt that the infant thrives on love. Countless studies of the development of infants have shown that love and care are vital. But caring should not be mistaken for reaction and constant supervision. Show care and affection in situations when it is natural, such as eating and nursing, when it is natural to create a you-and-I situation, when it is natural to nurse, sing, chat, and get to know each other. The rest of the time it is important to leave the infant in peace and quiet to sleep or, when awake, to get to know herself without constant intervention from her surroundings. Often it is very difficult to show the infant this respect and leave her alone. Constantly satisfying your own need for reassurance and your need to look at your beautiful baby will often influence the infant's ability to be content with herself. Too many disturbances quickly lead to dependence on constant attention from the surroundings, and a vicious cycle of bad habits is created. By giving the infant peace and quiet for the first months of her life, she will get used to her physical life; the crying will gradually stop, and the baby may start to sleep during the night without waking up at all hours.

When awake, the infant will begin to test her voice and smile; she will reach out and look around. At this stage, the infant needs no toys, for she has more than enough to interact with in herself and her parent or care giver.

What Environment Should We Offer the Infant?

An infant needs as much quiet as possible: no loud intrusive sounds from radio and television, no mechanical noise, no unnecessary transportation, etc. Warmth is needed so that the infant does not use energy for maintaining her body temperature. Try to avoid strong light. Attend to the infant's physical needs with love and calmness.

Nurture the infant's skin. Give the infant freedom of movement. Make sure her clothes offer ample room for movement. Adapt food to her requirements and growth.

If you have attended to the above, there is probably no reason to worry about crying. Make a quiet check; tucking the infant back in her bed lovingly will give sufficient signals from the care giver to assure the infant that you are close at hand and that everything is all right. This gives the message that it is all right that she is learning to become comfortable with her body and getting to know herself better. Through unnecessary attention, the infant becomes dependent on attention and on the adult's attendance to her own needs. The more restless the adults are, the more restless the children will be. The less we disturb the infant, the better chance she has of adapting to her life on earth. The first month, indeed the first couple of months, have a profound influence on the development of the individuality. This is the time when the foundation upon which all else will rest is formed: the creation of inner peace and psychological equilibrium.

Development of Motor Skills in the First Year

Observing the infant's movements requires a strong will, because it is difficult not to interfere. Children develop quite individually. Some are quick, others are slow. It is very important to respect the child's own pace and avoid comparisons with other children. It is important to realize that the infant has no need for toys of any kind. The infant has himself, and it is by observing himself and his limbs that the infant develops. That is why the infant should not be offered any toys.

First Quarter

The newborn baby lies on his back with arms and legs bent and clenched hands. His head is turned slightly to one side (note that he has a favorite side!), and the body/head alignment is asymmetrical. First, the infant will move his eyes. Open and close, open and close; slowly the infant looks at his surroundings after the initial squint and the ability to focus is trained. Then comes the head. The child follows the sounds with his head. The better the child becomes at orienting himself, often the larger is the resulting bald spot which develops on the back of the head.

The rest of the body is still completely uncoordinated. Sudden jerky movements may occur, but no coordinated, conscious movements. If frightened, the whole body will jerk, and at first he will seek a large surface. Arms and legs go out, and then he curls up in fetal position. The hands and arms start to wave about in the air; the movements are not coordinated. Often he will wave an arm in front of his eyes, which are now under more and more control.

Second Quarter

The infant gains more and more control of her head movements. Hands are observed with growing interest. Movements with the hands are repeated. The infant can now lift her hands up in front of her eyes, and they are studied intensely. She opens and closes her hand of her own volition. She grips one hand with the other hand. It is easier to grip than to let go. The infant practices for weeks, until she masters the skill. Later come legs and toes, which can even be put in the mouth. This takes a much shorter time than the hands. The infant likes to suck everything.

The infant becomes conscious of her sides and starts to turn. She reaches out towards her surroundings. If the infant is in a cot with bars, she attempts to reach the bars. A small cloth with a woolen head is moved, tasted, dropped, again and again. Side, back, side, it is difficult to balance. The infant supports herself by using her head, shoulders, arms, hands, and legs to remain in balance. The movements are repeated again and again, until the infant can lie on her side. This also gives the infant a new perspective within her field of vision.

Once the infant finds balance, her development continues. One day the infant will fall over and land on her stomach. She is lying in a very awkward position, with one arm caught under her body. Often she will start to cry. If the parent does not intervene, the infant will find a way to release the arm and get back on her back. If you help, the child must necessarily repeat the exercise again and again, as she must learn to move the arm herself. It is part of any development that things take time, and only by constant repetition will the infant develop her skills. An infant will always seek to lie on the back; in the bath, for example, if you turn the infant on her stomach, she will quickly attempt to turn around onto the back.

The infant is now getting used to lying on her stomach. She lifts her head, learns to use her hands and arms. The legs are often floating in the air, the bottom is planted solidly on the ground. The infant begins to stretch. She moves to reach things, and gets closer to her goal. She bends and stretches and sheds her asymmetrical body alignment. The back is straightened. The limbs become flexible and muscular. This takes months.

Third Quarter

The infant starts to roll: from the back, to the stomach, returning to the back. Arms, legs and head are tested; he reaches for things and grasps them.

Fourth Quarter

The infant begins to crawl. Up on the arms, bend the knees, wobble, push backwards and, finally, push forwards. The emphasis is on either the legs or the arms.

Physical Development in the First Year

Once the infant learns to crawl, it can be difficult to keep up while walking alongside! How the infant develops his crawl is not a matter of chance. If he has any weaknesses, he will strengthen them by exercising those muscles again and again. This is why infants with weak backs will require a long period on their stomachs to strengthen the back, followed by a long crawling period. There is no need to worry; they will get up. They simply need more time to get their bodies ready.

It is important that the child have sufficient space to develop, and the parent should monitor his development carefully. We must be very patient; some children need more time than others.

It is important not to compare the child with other children, but to compare him with himself a couple of months ago and look at the development that has taken place in the intervening time. This is the only way of gauging the development of the individual child.

Sitting

Sitting correctly is a very economical position. It is a sitting movement. The body weight rests on the lower end of the back. The back is straight, the head balanced. The infant does not get tired from sitting in this position. At the same time it is a mobile position, and the infant can turn in all directions without losing his balance.

An incorrect sitting position is one in which the back is bent, the breast and rib cage exert pressure on the inner organs. Breathing is difficult. The infant can fall over at any moment. The infant moves constantly, and will naturally change position between sitting and lying down; in this process it uses the entire body.

When children are held upright, put in seats, strollers or similar forced sitting positions before they are ready for it, they do not have the opportunity to follow their own developmental sequences and, most importantly, their own pace. One can see the stress under which the child's back is put in such situations.

Pulling up to Stand

At the end of the first year the child starts to stand, often by using the strength of his arms. This is not a sudden thing. The progression of motor skills follows a set and lawful pattern. Certain steps of this progression happen very quickly and are difficult to observe, whereas other steps may be attempted by the child, who then gives up for lack of success. The sequence of movements develops from lying on his back, to side, stomach, knees, and then to crawling. Once the infant can roll onto his stomach, it will be about five to six months before he can stand by himself.

When the infant balances on his side, supporting himself with an arm, he can start to sit. When the infant kneels, he can get up into a standing position by holding on to something.

Often the infant tries to stand before he can sit. From a kneeling position he holds on and drags himself up to a standing position. He uses his hands to grip, his arm muscles to hold on, and his stomach for support; he can hardly support himself on his feet. When the child is tired, he lets go and falls down, or clutches onto something and cries. Again, it is important to help slowly. If the infant falls, the impact is often very small. The child wants to do it his own way and he can do it. He will repeat the movements again and again until he masters them, if we do not take away his initiative. When the child begins to stand, he also supports himself slightly on the legs. He often stands on his toes with legs wide apart, falls down, crawls forwards, tries again, and so on.

Standing Alone

Learning to stand alone may take months. It takes a lot of practice to evolve from four legs to two. Balance on the back legs, fall down on the hands. Then stand alone for a few seconds. Often the infant stands alone with toys in her hand without knowing it, and then falls when she becomes conscious of the situation. Once the child stands alone, she may start to walk.

It may take 4-6 months from the time that the infant begins to stand till she learns to walk. It is important to give the child this time, and the parent or care giver should not interfere out of pure eagerness to accelerate her development. The child will continue to alternate between standing, walking, falling, and crawling.

Nøkken

Walking Alone

Usually the child will walk in the first half of her second year, with legs wide apart, feet turned inward, rolling a bit like a sailor, with arms held out for balance. The feet grip the ground, taking small steps, and the knees are often lifted high. This lasts for only a few days; then the child adapts his walk. The weaker the child's muscles are, the longer he will take to gain control. Again, it is important to leave the child alone so that he may pace himself and strengthen weaker body parts. Usually this includes feet, knees, and hips. The child "observes" his own development intensely. The child experiments. He makes a huge effort to become familiar with details. Repetition is pure pleasure. The child can play for months with each new movement for the first year or two.

Every child has his own history of development. The method is far more important to the child than the result. The learning process is significant for his whole life. Through the process the child learns independence, patience, endurance, and the ability to concentrate his attention on one thing.

Emmi Pikler's work has been a substantial reference for this chapter. The North American center for her work is in Los Angeles, founded by Magda Gerber. For information about this work, please contact RIE (Resources for Infant Educarers) at www.rie.org / educarer@rie.org. Videos, training opportunities, and other information are available.

CHAPTER 2

The Child-Care Center Nøkken and Its Environment

Based on this understanding of a child's development, which takes time and must be given time, I find it difficult to care for children under walking age. Having several children together would create too much disturbance for infants, who need peaceful surroundings. The care requirements are also very high. Attention to individual needs is very difficult with many infants.

In other words, I am ignoring child-care needs in a country like Denmark, where maternity leave is only six months. It is obvious that a solution must be found to meet this need, but finding a solution that meets the requirements of both the labor market and the child would be very difficult. Legislation in Denmark allows an additional maternity leave period of six to twelve months, with the right to return to your old job. However, the benefit for this additional six to twelve months period is only 70% of that of the initial six months' period. One possibility might be for child-care centers to work with trained caregivers, who could look after the infant's needs for peace and quiet and a lot of care in their own homes. This would involve the creation of a local network around the child-care center which could cater to different needs.

Nøkken

This particular subject is overdue for closer study. Nøkken has set its minimum age at walking age. The child must be able to walk away from her mother and into the world on her own.

We are open for six hours, from 8:30 am to 2:30 pm. Our idea is that we share the children with their parents. We look after the children for six hours, the parents have them for six waking hours and the children sleep for twelve hours. In other words, the family will still exert influence on the child's development. The staff at the center does not change during the day: we are all there to say good morning and all there to say goodbye. There are no overlapping shifts: we all know how the others are feeling. It gives the child an important sense of continuity and security. She is not disturbed by comings and goings. The working hours are just long enough for the staff members to be able to smile when they leave after a non-stop working day. There are no coffee breaks; the adults are in constant activity with tasks that are worthy of imitation. In our experience, you cannot do this for more than six hours. Inasmuch as we work with children from walking age to school age (seven years), we cover an incredible variety of developmental stages. It is easier to accommodate children developing at different rates. There is lots of room for a three- or four-year-old who walks more slowly, because the one-year-olds will always be slower, and he can walk with them when we are out on our daily walk, for example. It is a great advantage for an only child who, through caring for younger children, can gain an insight into interaction with other age groups. Only by offering them the possibility of natural imitation do children learn how to nurture. Since all the adults know all the children, this means that no one has to adapt to new ways of doing things, which is reassuring for the children; they do not need to use energy in reacting to different attitudes, opinions, or ways of doing things.

It is obviously difficult. Parents often need longer opening hours, while at the same time they want the world's best early-childhood program with a motivated and relaxed staff. This is a difficult task and, knowing that we cannot accommodate all needs, we have chosen to favor the children. It is a conscious choice we have made as a child-care center. Most of our parents also have to make a choice. They change jobs, reduce their working hours, or work flexible hours: the solutions are many and varied as they consciously choose to spend a lot of time with their children. There are obvious consequences, mainly financial, but it is a conscious choice. It also means that our parents are very involved with their children, which allows for strong cooperation between parents and the center.

The aim of the child-care center is to resemble an extended family as much as possible, to have surroundings that look like home, and to have activities and chores that are normal to home life. The reason is that, in my view, child-care centers have taken on a completely new role in the past couple of years. In previous years, children attended a child-care center for social stimulation, to participate in activities that the family could not offer. The child-care centers supplemented the homes. Industrialization, women's entry into the work force (women have always worked, but their work has never been valued in socioeconomic terms), and women's liberation meant that children had to be away from home for longer hours. The quick mechanization of the home environment with washing machines, dishwashers, all kinds of electrical appliances, and, most recently, the introduction of fast food, seems to have reversed the role of child-care centers. The centers must now teach children the basics to help them achieve the necessary skills to choose their life style at a later stage. The parents' role is mainly to stimulate and organize activities of a social and/or cultural interest.

If we take as our starting point the assumption that children come to the kindergarten to learn fundamental skills so that they will later be in a position to take hold of their own daily lives, we must necessarily create a daily life situation that takes these requirements into consideration. What good is it to be told all the time in childhood that one should take care of the natural world if you have never really been in it, never known the seasons, or known through your own experience that a bud will become a leaf, a fruit, or food for eating?

Only through daily participation does the child take part in the creation of her life. Only by being surrounded by adults engaged in ordinary activities, doing chores with happiness and seriousness, will the child be able to relate to the important tasks in life, namely to develop and improve, not just for her own sake, but also for others. As a result, everything we do at Nøkken has a purpose. We make sure that all work processes have been carefully prepared. We ensure that they have a start, a middle, and an end. This pattern is characteristic of all things great and small. Through this the children get the opportunity to take part in the whole process. They learn through participation how things work in practice — not by words, but by action.

Staff Relations

We need to have a very close relationship to be able to work together. We must be open about our views and ideas. We have weekly evening meetings where we read together and discuss different aspects of our work: children, parents, daily work, etc. We also have a study group one evening every other week. There are staff meetings for all Waldorf child-care staff in the Sjaelland area once a month; there are bazaar evenings with parents and parent conferences, plus all the evenings spent decorating for the seasonal celebrations (at least 10 a year). I can safely say that it takes a great deal of commitment to work at our child-care center, and it is really more a lifestyle than just work. The children feel the enthusiasm, and hopefully it gives them an impression of motivated adults. It is important for the care giver to know his or her own limits, so that what should be enriching does not turn into complete exhaustion.

Nøkken

Number of Children

We aim to have 24 to 26 children in the group. Often there are more, because demand is great and we just cannot say no. Our upper limit is definitely 30 children. The 30th child seems like five children! I have difficulty coping with more than 30 children and acknowledging every child on a daily basis. We also want to keep our garden looking like a garden, and with too many little feet, it is difficult to maintain our garden with flowers, vegetables, and grass.

One-third of our children are under the age of three and two-thirds are over three. There are about four children in each age group. As a result, there are never more than four or five children leaving the center at one time to go on to school and, consequently, never more new children than that. This makes it easier for everyone. Brothers and sisters have first priority, although this rule creates havoc from time to time, because brothers and sisters have a tendency to be born when it suits them! But so far it has never been a problem. We like to say that change creates happiness and that everything comes to those who can wait, or otherwise you just get on with yourself.

We also find it is important for the whole group to be together: even the "difficult" six-year-olds will demonstrate their sense of care when they look into the eyes of a one-year-old and see the need for a helping hand. The young children learn to play through observing the older children. Being left alone to look at other children playing is the best way to learn. An adult can never and should never play like a child. The adult should be around, engaged in adult activities and not be a playmate. The adult may initiate play, but must at all times be conscious of his or her role and know when to leave the children to play on their own terms. Children should not depend on adults to participate in their games nor on adult attitudes. Free play will come from the children's own imagination, inspired by adults' working, songs, and stories, as well as everyday events.

The mixed age group benefits all the children, because the greater the age range, the easier it is to find a perfect match, and this spans all age groups.

Daily Rhythm: Inhaling/Exhaling

Our first priority is to spend most of the day outdoors. We spend five out of the six hours we are together outdoors. In Denmark, where you have so-called bad weather 60% of the time, it can be hard to understand why we don't all emigrate to New Zealand. But since we are living here, I consider it important to learn to live with our weather. As a result, all weather is good weather if you are dressed for it. Nature also offers us the most natural physical challenges. Our center is located in the middle of a capital city. More than half the children live in small apartments.

Nøkken

Most playgrounds are boring, dirty, and often full of things to which the children find it hard to relate. This means that life at home is usually indoors or involves indoor activities (gym, swimming, and the like). The toddler needs to exercise. He needs to use his whole body, to explore all possibilities. The toddler needs to climb, run, balance, jump around. He cannot do this indoors. Of course, child centers in other parts of the world in other climates with children from other surroundings may need to have other activities in their programs, but that is the exciting thing about working with child care: the challenges are where you are, and it is a question of finding out which needs you are able to meet based on the possibilities at your disposal. Children's needs basically remain the same, but meeting them remains the responsibility of the care giver.

Living in a country where it gets darker and darker in winter and lighter and lighter in summer gives a very varied seasonal rhythm. Being enriched by four major seasons means that two days are never alike and the changes happen before our very eyes. We are out every day on our daily walk, keeping in touch with nature's changes, watching the geese arrive in spring, smelling the coming of spring. We feel the earth breathing in a physical sense, and there is no doubt that the children learn to appreciate nature. They don't need intellectual explanations about the coming of spring or the wind blowing. They can feel it; it is a completely natural thing to them, and with this understanding of nature they learn from Mother Nature herself to care for her. When adults look after their surroundings, the children follow their example, not in words, but by deeds.

Having a garden is almost a basic right for a child; a garden which offers lots of hiding places where the children can find peace from curious eyes; where for once, the child is completely free and alone. Our children are surrounded by lots of fruit trees, berry bushes, sand pits, a hen house, rabbit cages, a pigeon house, a vegetable garden, an herb garden, flower beds, and a laundry area, all offering the children ample opportunities for hiding or changing games all the time, while the adults are working in the garden without interfering in the world of play. The adult is, however, close enough to know what is going on and can speak with the children if things get out of hand.

In a country where it rains a lot, it is important to focus on the good things about rain. Dressed properly, it is wonderful for all ages to play in the rain. Jumping in puddles, splashing through the rain, and building dams turns rainy weather into a wonderful experience when you are allowed to play with a natural resource that you should really attempt to conserve in your daily life.

Being outdoors also means that there is more space for the individual. There are no ceilings; the noise level rarely becomes unbearable. Children who need to putter quietly about can do so without being disturbed by those requiring more physically demanding games.

Our "sleepers" sleep outdoors in an open shed, wrapped in woolen blankets according to the season. This is quite common in Denmark, or at least it

Nøkken

used to be. Sleep is important and with all the exercise and the good food, the children look forward to their nap: it is enjoyable, and they need a rest.

Living outdoors means that our children are rarely ill. From time to time, all of them go through a longer period of illness, but the infections — running noses, coughs, stomach, and eye infections — are rarely seen here. Obviously, it varies from child to child, but overall they are very healthy.

One might imagine that there would be few outdoor adult tasks that the children could emulate in the physical environment at Nøkken. But if you are living and working, as we are, in an old house and garden, there is constant repair work to be carried out. The compost heap needs turning to give new nourishment to the vegetable garden; the animals need feeding, and their "stables" must be kept clean. Every day there are lots of fruit, berries, and vegetables to be washed. In other words, there are lots of chores that are easily done outdoors. Only your own imagination sets limits.

I also feel that it is important for the children to be indoors. After our daily walk, we go inside to eat. With red cheeks and a healthy appetite, the children eat their warm porridge, pie, or soup. There are no picky eaters here, because everybody has the same food to eat and does so happily. Before we eat, we light candles on each table for the sun, the moon, and all the stars that blink at us and show us the way at night. Then we sing a song, give thanks for the food on our table, and we eat. Once we have finished eating, we sing another song about being content and happy. Then we all get up and help clear the table. While we are clearing the table, the children play indoors until it is story time. The story, an old folk tale, will be told after the youngest children have been put to bed. In other words, the indoor activities are concentrated in the kitchen and the work taking place in the kitchen. The kitchen still plays a central role in our daily life.

A Day in the Life ...

Our child-care center is composed of three houses. I live with my three children in the largest of the houses. It is very important to the children that there is a heart beating in the center all day and night. It is a real home, requiring a lot of care. In the basement, there is a cloakroom for the five- to seven-year-olds and a toilet. In a back room, there is a shop where the parents can buy bio-dynamic products. Bread arrives from the Aurion bakery every Wednesday, vegetables from bio-dynamic farms every Tuesday, and other purchases of various bio-dynamic products arrive when we have sold out or new demands arise.

We can also order woolen underwear and clothing to sell for the children. In this way, parents have the opportunity to buy these products without difficulty and at affordable prices, as the store operates on a cooperative basis. The children shop with their parents in the little store and see them buying the products they already know from the center. Many of their food dislikes vanish, because they know themselves how much they eat at the center. By giving them the very best products, we also avoid many allergies. Here are no additives, no unnecessary use of sugar, and all products are of high quality. The children are also used to visiting a farm every spring, where we go to sow our own grain together with the farmer, and we return to harvest it together in autumn. This shows the children the connection between the food they eat and the place that produces it. An opportunity

is created to build a bridge between consumers and producers. The world makes sense.

The entrance to the center is at the corner of a busy street and a quiet street. Three hundred feet on each side we have access to huge recreational areas, although we are only a fifteen-minute bicycle ride from the center of Copenhagen! The children use the corner entrance gate when they come in the morning, and they leave the kindergarten by the gate at my house. Again, the idea is to establish a routine so that the children know exactly what is happening.

The center's main building is an old timber house of approximately 600 square feet, with an open kitchen and living area, and a room used for playing and story-telling. Upstairs are two rooms used by trainees and visitors. There are a laundry and a toilet in an annex. Only wood is used for heating. It is a very primitive, but extremely cozy house, just what we need. It is old and in constant need of repair; it keeps changing. The center has just bought the house with funds saved over the years.

The center is on a quarter-acre plot of land. The plot is planted with vegetable gardens and fruit trees. We have 25 fruit trees, including apple, pear, plum, and cherry. They are old fruit trees, and they don't grow tall. They give fruit at different times of the year, and therefore we have fresh fruit over a long period. We usually have enough to store some for winter. The crowns of the trees offer shelter, a kind of ceiling. In the garden we also have berry bushes, a vegetable garden, flower beds, an herb garden, and a sand pit.

There is also a hen house with a rooster and several hens. The hens are not pets. We keep them mainly to give our city children a chance to be in close proximity to animals and so that they can see where eggs come from. They also give the children an opportunity to show care in looking after the hens. The hen house needs cleaning, and the hens like to be fed with dandelions and other greens which we find on our walks. Any food not eaten by the children is given to the hens, so here the children see that everything is used and nothing is thrown away. This is something

Nøkken

we express not verbally, but through our actions, and that is a language children understand. Sometimes the fox takes the hens, and we have to start all over again, but that is all part of nature. Children are not sentimental; they are very practical.

Our front garden is used to store firewood. There is also a wood shed, but the firewood is stacked and split in the front yard. Every spring the wood man comes with four to five cords of firewood. The logs have already been sawn up, but we still  have to stack the wood in our shed and, to some extent, split it. Firewood day is a big day. Many of the fathers take half a day off from their work to help. All the children help to the best of their ability: one carries a single piece of wood, another stacks them high in her arms, and others use wheelbarrows. We get sweaty and laugh a lot, and, wow, aren't the fathers strong! The children love to see their parents' enthusiasm. They often talk about firewood day during the year: "Do you remember when Asger drove the wheelbarrow full of firewood right up to the trees? Or when Kaare stacked the wood to the top of the shed?" But, most importantly, the firewood reminds us of spring. The smell of the wood chips, the sweat, the sense of togetherness, of a job well done — they are valuable experiences indeed.

We use only firewood for heating. It enables the children to relate to the element of fire. In modern homes with electric stoves, electric lamps, and central heating, most families don't use fire at all, and the child doesn't understand the origin of heat. By using only firewood for heating, it becomes part of our everyday life. Every day we split firewood and fetch firewood, and every day we light the fire. The temperature in our house depends on our ability to keep the fire going.

Most of our seasonal events take place in the garden. This is symbolized by — among other things — a spiral of oak wood embedded in the ground.

For the celebration of the Advent spiral, we invite the parents to come early in the morning. The Advent spiral is covered with spruce, and in the middle is a large plant pot holding a lighted candle. The light reflects in the white frost on the spruce. Singing, each child in turn walks to the center, lights his candle and walks all the way out again. Then the parents may light their candles, if they so wish.

Afterwards, we all go into the Nøkkehus and drink warm fruit juice with nuts, raisins, and fresh buns. When we have finished eating, the children take out their harvest wreaths and, together with parents and teachers, we make an Advent wreath using the spruce which we have secretly brought in from outside.

Nøkken

The spiral in the garden is more than just a spiral; it is a main feature of our seasonal events, and in that way it forms part of the children's games.

There are Easter eggs hanging in one of the plum trees. Usually, the last egg from the previous year's celebration drops as the new year's Easter is drawing close. Thus, the garden participates in the seasons on different levels, both in its own way and in the way we use it to celebrate the year.

When the children arrive between 8:30 and 9:00 in the morning, they are always met by one of the staff (usually the same person). First, we wish the parent good morning and shake hands. Then we shake hands with the child. It is very important for the care giver and the child to meet, to establish a bridge of faith by shaking hands. A handshake may also give an important indication of any problems. Is the hand warm or cold, sweaty or dry, shaky or steady, and so on? Looking each other openly in the eye and showing confidence are important qualities in life. The handshake is the bridge that is a way of saying, without words, that now I will do my best to look after you until your mom or dad picks you up again. It is a question of faith to meet the world and take up this challenge. A simple "hello" can never replace this. By shaking hands with all the children we also know who has come in.

To begin with, many parents find it a bit old-fashioned to shake hands. But after a while they feel comfortable with it, and often tell us how they have started shaking hands with their own friends. Without really thinking about it, they put out their hands, and very few people ignore this opportunity to exchange handshakes. This is something I see very strongly in the infant. If you offer a child something in an open gesture, it is in the nature of the child to take and give back.

After being welcomed, the children hang up their backpacks. Then it's time to start playing. The parents only stay for a short while. We don't want them to stay longer, because now it's time for social interaction with friends, and the parents do not participate in this.

The kindergarten is in full swing before the first child appears at the gate. Staff members start work fifteen minutes before opening time. We gather outside in an open shed and read from the works of Rudolf Steiner. Then we quickly go through the program for the day, including any special activities, and mention absent children. Parents must call between 7:45 and 8:15 if their children are not coming. Special activities include birthdays, etc. Then we each start our work. The tasks have been divided among the staff at our staff meetings, so we all know what to do. Laundry is hung out to dry every day.

Nøkken

The children are welcome to participate in the tasks according to ability, and we do not encourage them verbally, but by action. When a tiny toddler participates, it is often by a very small imitating action. It is important to interpret this correctly and to respect that the child is going through the movements inwardly, although outwardly there are few signs. By letting the one-year-old perceive what is happening without encouraging or commenting on his actions, the door is opened for the child to do things his own way, and slowly he learns things in much the same way as when he was a tiny infant who had to discover his own hand.

The child must learn for himself, and through observation acquires the tools to go out into the world. If the child was in a garden where the adults did not work, how could he learn from imitation? The result would often be senseless running around and teasing. When you come to a place where you feel that everyone is busy, you are carried along on a stream of activity. This appeals to a child and his senses. Children live by their will, by action, and when meaningful tasks form the basis of their daily lives, a foundation is formed to allow them to understand and evaluate the tasks and use them as building blocks for their future experiences.

It can be difficult for a toddler to say goodbye to his parents. A pet is an ideal link. Our Angora rabbit, Thumper, inspires confidence with his warmth and peace. Once a child is busy looking after Thumper, feeding him dandelion leaves or something similar, the sadness of parting from the parents is soon forgotten. If the parents have a good feeling about their child in the center, it is easier for the child to let go. It is almost impossible to look after a child if the parents aren't able to let go. That is why I think it is important that they believe that our center is, if not the best in the world, then at least the second best, so that the parents feel good about leaving their children with us and are confident that we will do our very best for the child while they are busy at work. Once the child senses that the parents are happy, saying goodbye seldom creates any problems.

Back to Thumper. Thumper isn't just a pet; Thumper also gives us lovely Angora wool which we shear, card, spin, and use for knitting. This is a process the children take part in, and it gives them a knowledge of how to make clothes — again, not expressed in words, but in action.

It is very important to us that the child-care center resembles a home as much as possible and that we enjoy the uniqueness of having siblings together. This is not because siblings spend more time with each other than with their other playmates, but because it creates a sense of security and encourages more tolerance than normal. To join as a brother or sister is very easy. They are practically born into it. All of us have known the child all his life and followed his development. The parents know the center, so the initial phase is very easy. Knowing that there is always room for siblings also gives the parents peace of mind.

Nøkken

I should also mention that the staff members have their own children in the kindergarten, which presents very few problems because we can discuss everything at our staff meetings. We also ensure that the older children are not supervised by their own mothers all the time. By making it possible for the staff members to have their own children here, we overcome any feelings of guilt the staff may have regarding their own children. If the staff members are unhappy with their own role as mothers, it creates major problems in their home environment which will then be transferred to the kindergarten. We don't need guilt.

At 9 am, all the children gather around the spiral. Now it's time for the day to start in earnest. All the children should have arrived by 9 o'clock. There may be the odd dental appointment, but the main rule is that we start at 9 am. It is important to set a fixed time. The children need to know who is present so that they can play without being disturbed. In this way, they learn that things have a start, that it is important to be present, that it does matter whether you are there or not. A daily rhythm which remains unchanged is very important for children.

When we gather everyone for the morning circle, it is done by quietly repeating, "It's time to sing," and the children come from all corners of the garden. The toddlers are often already there because instinctively they know exactly when things are going to happen, through daily repetition. Everybody joins hands and forms a circle. Here we all stand together ready for a new day. In all kinds of weather. Holding hands. Young and old. Now the day begins. You can feel it in the air.

We sing a song from the "High School Song Book," a treasured Danish song book, a song that describes the season. We sing the same song for two weeks. The reason that we have chosen this song book is that many of the parents know these wonderful songs and can sing with their children at home. After the song, we sing a good morning to everyone. In this way, every individual is mentioned and is for a short time the center of attention. Then we sing to whomever is not there, so that nobody is left out. In conclusion, we sing a pentatonic song. The toddlers cannot stand still much longer, and we sing, "You may go to the gate." Everybody rushes to the gate. We have a pram for the youngest children so that they don't have to walk all the way. There are two in each pram, always the same together, so that they know exactly what is happening. It is individual how far they walk on their own, but it rarely takes long before they are familiar with the walk and want to run or walk by themselves.

Outside the gate, which is opened only by an adult, we wait until we are all ready. We have to cross a very busy road, and so it requires a lot of attention.

Nøkken

When we are ready, the same adult will go into the road and ask the children to cross. The children know all the walks. It rarely takes us long to get to a special place where we stay for about an hour.

The children don't have to walk in pairs, but are allowed to move freely on the pavement. There is always an adult in front, one or two in the middle and one at the back. The pram is in the middle. This gives us an opportunity to let them fulfill their individual exercise requirements. Some run, and some walk slowly. We don't have to hurry them along; there is no stress, except that we all have to get to the special place and stay off the road. As none of the adults would even think of walking on the road — to pass, for instance — the children never do it. It goes without saying that we keep an eye on every child: we take no unnecessary risks. Along our walks, there are fixed stops. If the older children get there first, they would not dream of going past such a point. They have stopped here all their lives, and they know that this is as far as they are allowed to go. They help by teaching the younger children, again, not by saying "you mustn't do that," but by example, by holding hands with them and waiting patiently, or by playing with whatever is available until we are ready to continue.

Once we have reached our special spot, we stay there for about an hour. The weather usually determines where we go. In the summer we often go to the nearby marsh area teeming with bird life. There are tall rushes to hide in, new areas to explore, lots of animal tracks (in particular from "bears" and "wolves"

Nøkken and Its Environment

that only live in our imagination). There are small hills to roll down and water holes to look at. When it is windy, in particular in autumn and winter, we go to a large cemetery nearby. It is huge and park like. We have favorite spots with hardly any graves. There are many really tall and beautiful trees. The gardeners allow us to climb some of the trees, because they know that we will be very careful. The gardeners are our best friends. They show us how trees are felled when they are old and sick, they show us how necessary it is to look after nature and, not least, they are men who feel strongly about their work. Many of our gardeners are men of few words, but big hearts. They allow the children to learn for themselves, they understand that we need branches for our seasonal celebrations, and they are always helpful. The boys latch on to the gardeners like greedy fledglings. We all agree that our gardeners are simply the best.

In the churchyard there are also lots of bushes in which to hide. Nature gives us all the toys we need: fruits, cones, sticks, leaves, and rain puddles. There is free rein for our imagination. A stick becomes a boat, which becomes a knight, who in turn changes into a hunter. Only our imagination sets limits. Children are sense beings and nature enlivens them, allows them to gain experience. The small children don't play together, but beside each other. There is enough room for everyone. They can go in and out of each other's games.

The youngest children often want to be left alone, alone with their senses. Maybe they'll touch the tree bark, find a bug, feel the wind in their cheeks, or just be. If we do not respect their need for peace, but are busy sharing our experiences and feelings with them, we deny the child the right to gain his own experience, at his own pace, in his own way. By giving the child space, we show respect for the child's individuality, give him the opportunity to develop at his own tempo, and, most importantly, learn to know himself. Some children require a very long time. The peace they achieve by being left to their own senses, by experiencing that

being alone is all right, gives them an incredible ballast later in life. The child is capable of managing on his own and is not afraid of being alone. The adult's most important task is to leave the child alone.

Allowing a child to make his own observations, use his senses, and explore by himself doesn't mean that there is no room for us. The adult should always be nearby to offer help, if necessary, but it is important to hold back and not expect the child to fulfill any needs we may have as adults or parents.

Children under the age of four cannot be expected to play together; they play beside each other. They cannot resume the games of yesterday. They are not very social; they live on their own terms. This is why it is important to offer them a framework where they are not pressed into doing things for which they are not ready. By having lots of space and opportunity to observe older children at play, they learn to play. They imitate everything they see in their own way. They are not in doubt that they are a hunter, a dog, or a squirrel, or all three at the same time. It is very important that the child doesn't do things for which she is too young. It might be tempting to help the child climb a tree if she cannot manage on her own. If you do that, you will also have to help her down again, and you are making the child rely on help.

If the child has to wait until she can manage on her own, you can be sure that she will not climb up before she can get down again. How exhilarating to have watched the older children climb the trees and then suddenly one day be able to do it yourself. Often the adult interferes too quickly, and then the child withdraws. Out of sheer kindness it can be tempting to suggest this and that, or maybe to discuss it with the other children (this is the worst thing you can do) and make it incredibly hard for the child to get back in. There are times in a child's life when she needs peace and quiet. The child cannot express her emotions in words. She may say that the others are all stupid, or that she is bored; her body looks dejected. If your attitude is that it is all right to be bored, it helps the child tremendously when the adult doesn't continue to focus on the situation. One day it is all over, the child comes out of her chrysalis (maybe she has got her six-year-old molars) and has completely forgotten that she was once bored and cannot understand what you are talking about if you refer to this period. Again it is important for the adult

Nøkken

to keep track of the child's development so that one is not living yesterday today, and so that tomorrow can be a new day.

Understanding the child's development is a good tool for understanding children who may have had problems of some kind. Before a child starts at Nøkken, we visit the home one evening after the child has gone to bed. We ask the parents to tell us about the pregnancy, the birth, and the time before the child is due to join us.

I take private notes on anything that may have influenced the development of the child's motor skills. It is a special feeling for the parents to share their observations. We then tell them about the kindergarten, and they ask a lot of questions. We may not even always have a reply.

This way I know a lot about the individual child. If the child has not crawled as a baby, I try to create situations where that is possible. By first letting some older children crawl over any obstacles, the younger children will soon follow. One little boy, for example, had never crawled, but once he got started, he tried again and again, until he suddenly got up, with shining eyes, and walked happily away. Now that bit was over and done with, and he was very pleased with himself.

A child comes running along. There is a stone in the way and the child falls.

A "normal" reaction from the adult would often be to run quickly to his side with bated breath, with many questions as to what happened and how bad it was, as well to express anxiety about the fall. The child's reaction is often geared to the adult's reaction rather than to the event, the fall. The same is true of crying. If the adults restrain their anxiety and simply observe the situation, the child's reaction will often be quite different. It is important to realize that a child will fall thousands of times because by falling he learns to get up, trains his balance, and learns his own limitations.

Crying because of a fall is all right. Crying is a means of expression. The child was frightened, maybe it hurt a little, but then that's it. Up again. If the adult stays back and observes the situation from the sidelines, the child is offered an opportunity to handle the situation his own way and to learn from it. Maybe it was pleasant to look at the clouds, or to brush the fingers, count them and regard the fall as an experience linked with new experiences, instead of being locked in the original fright by a caring adult. I am not saying that we should ignore a child falling and not act, if necessary. What I am saying is to wait, give the child the opportunity to learn from the event, so that he matures through experience. The more we mix our confused emotions with the children's, the less independent they become.

Nøkken

Singing is one of the best ways of talking with children. By singing, we step away from ourselves. The voice becomes "neutral," "I" becomes part of a community. The small children love to sing and rhyme and make up nonsense words. On our walks we sing a lot. Exercising and singing is a wonderful thing. Often our children can sing before they can talk. As an example, I might mention a little boy we had. He knew very few words, and even then you had to know what they meant to understand him. Around Lantern time (in November) we sing lantern songs all the time, and one day we suddenly heard a new little voice singing all the words of the lantern song. It was little Asbjorn who could hardly speak, but who through song found a way to master speech. After the Lantern celebration, he quickly learned new words, and the parents were very relieved that there was nothing wrong with Asbjorn. He had just needed ample time to master speech.

We don't need to schedule a time for singing. We sing as much as we possibly can. Often we have singing games when we are out walking, and the children participate if they wish. If we (the adults) have a good day, all the children join in, otherwise we may have from eight to twenty participating. The younger children cannot really take part in the games, but they are often the keenest participants. The older children know that you cannot expect the same from them, so they will usually allow the toddlers to stop in mid-sentence or walk the wrong way around. Don't be fooled by young children who seem to be just looking. Often their eyes are glazed over, their expression is slightly vacant. In their minds, they are clearly participating.

If you disturb the child to encourage him to participate, he looks at you in bewilderment because he is already in the game, even if he is standing on the sidelines!

When you have always had the children, you know them very well, and they know you in return. Often you see your own gestures reflected in them. In one situation, for example, when an infant was crying, Adwoa (a six-year-old) was unhappy with our response and went to the child. Without a word, she sat down in front of the child, and made a protective gesture (a eurythmy "b") which allowed the child to leave her when he wished. At the same time, she turned her head sideways and looked elsewhere. The child immediately settled down and Adwoa continued on her way. The child got a non-verbal confirmation which said that someone is here if you need help, but it is also OK to cry; if you don't need me, I'll leave you alone.  Adwoa's gestures reflected the care she has received all her life. Here was an acceptance of herself which she expressed by showing her concern for the other child, while at the same time giving him the freedom to accept it or not.

When we get back from our walk at around 10:45, the young children are hungry. We divide the children into two groups. Children over the age of three go to the large Nøkkehus where they eat with two or three adults, always

Nøkken

the same people. The children have their own places at the table.

The children under the age of three go to the small Nøkkehus, a small timber building of about 150 square feet. It is heated with firewood only, and there is no electricity. It is like entering a cave. Outside, under the covered area where the children keep their backpacks, we get ready to hang up their coats and jackets. The children are helped in a special order. It is up to us not to be stressed by helping up to nine children. The adult, sitting on a low chair, greets the child with open arms. Adult and child work together to take off the child's coat. The child must know exactly what is happening all the time. The adult reaches out, offers to help pull a sleeve, the child accepts the gesture and together we get the arm out of the sleeve and so on. It may take considerable time to begin with, but the children are usually very cooperative. While this is happening, the others are looking and trying to imitate the process.

It is important that the situation is not perceived as an almost violent lightning-like attack. In these stressful situations, the parent often chooses not to take the time to teach the children to cooperate. However, the parent is after all in charge of the daily routine, so it is all a matter of planning. There doesn't

Nøkken and Its Environment

have to be stress in a child-care center; for we have the whole day at our disposal. By avoiding stress in the undressing situation, we have created an atmosphere of concentration which facilitates good digestion. By not talking while we are concentrating on the task, we create a sense of peace and calm. If the children know what is going on and what will be happening, they don't need to spend energy getting used to a new situation.

After taking her coat off, the child goes into the house and is greeted by another adult who is ready to greet her. First the child must find her indoor shoes in the basket and put them on. Then it is time to wash hands and dry them. The adult offers the child a towel and together they dry the hands.

Then the children sit down at their places at the table and wait for everyone to be seated. Often there is complete silence and one can almost feel the air of concentration. It is not that we are not allowed to talk; there often just isn't time.

Now a candle is lit for the sun and the moon and all the stars. We hold hands; sometimes some of the children are too young, and they just hold on to the nearest shirt. We sing a meal song, and then it is time to eat.

> *The Earth has given us bread,*
>
> *The Sun has given it life,*
>
> (The children hold hands at the table)
>
> *Dear Sun,*
>
> (Form arms like a round sun over the head)
>
> *Dear Earth,*
>
> (Form arms like a round earth at shoulder height)
>
> *Thanks are in our hearts,*
>
> (Cross hands over the chest
>
> and bend slightly forwards)
>
> *Blessed be our food.*

The food is served to each of the children individually, in their own pottery bowls. The size of the helping depends on the child. A child who eats a lot gets a medium-sized serving to ensure a break, and perhaps also a small spoon for smaller mouthfuls.

If a child has difficulty eating calmly and gobbles her food, we try to help by sitting next to the child and eating calmly ourselves. Instead of telling the child not to gobble her food, we touch her hand gently to reduce speed. We don't do it all the time, but just from time to time during the meal. In this way, the child is silently guided without being told that she is doing something wrong. This is how we always try to find ways to work with the child without telling her, because a child will always try to do her best.

The same method applies to drinking. If the child has ample time to lift her cup, she will succeed, especially if the adult doesn't worry about the cup being knocked over. If it is, so what? The child must learn from her own experience that the cup is empty and she is wet. There is a connection. Using plastic cups with rounded bottoms will only ensure that the child sees absolutely no connection between cause and effect. She will not learn from experience. The same goes for plastic bibs. They are practical, it's true, but the child doesn't understand that she will get wet if she spills, and it will take much longer for her to learn to eat properly.

When the meal is over and everyone is full, we sing a "thanks for the food" song. Then we leave the table to go over to the big house for potty time. After the

Nøkken

deep concentration of eating and digesting, there is an atmosphere of near-abandonment. In a corner of the kitchen the potties are taken out. The children take off their pants and diapers. Helping hands abound, because it is a difficult task. When everybody is seated, we sing nursery rhymes and finger songs. The children love them and they want them repeated again and again. There is nothing like hearing the same rhyme over and over again! Only the adult gets tired of repeating the same song or rhyme.

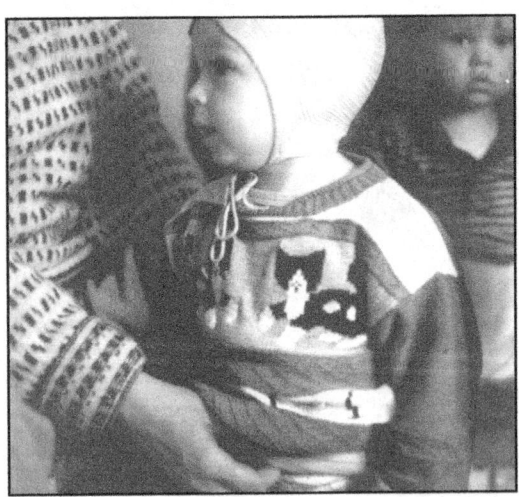

Now the same adult puts a diaper on each child, in the same order, paying attention to different needs. Some need to sleep longer and get to go to bed first; others just rest. By having time for the individual child, there is time to create a natural you-and-I situation. You feel the child's skin and body temperature. There's time for a cuddle if the child likes it, or at least a tickle. Close contact is in order; the child is a natural center of attention for a short time and enjoys it.

The same adult now puts the child in her usual cot or pram, which is in its usual place. The child brings her own bedclothes, washed at home, so that they smell of "mom." The child is tucked in, a silk scarf is placed over the cot or pram — partly to keep insects away, partly to soften the light.

Then it is time for a short verse:

> *Fourteen angels guard my bed*
> *two at my head*
> *two at my feet*
> *two at my right*
> *two at my left*
> *two cover me*
> *two wake me up*
> *two show me the way to paradise.*

Then we sing:

> *My guardian angel, please look after me*
> *day and night, early and late*
> *guard me forever and forever*
> *and I'll be happy, my guardian angel.*

We wish the child a good sleep, and the adult leaves her without any problems. When a child first comes to the center, there may be a little crying, but then we just stay close to the cot or go for a short walk with the pram until the child is asleep. This is always just for a very short initial period, because usually

Nøkken

the child is so full of impressions that she is looking forward to sleeping. We never secure the children in their beds. When they wake up, they call out or talk to themselves until they are taken out of bed. There is always an adult close by.

When the younger children are all tucked in, we get ready for story time in the big house. A low table is decorated with silk in many colors and, depending on the story, we add pebbles, branches, wooden animals or dolls made from wool,

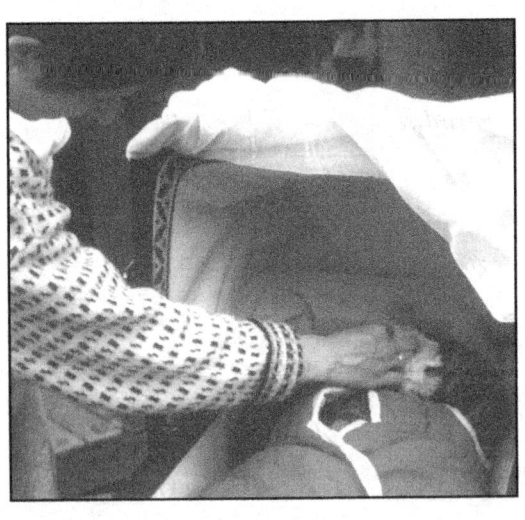

silk, or fabric. The children help. On the first day, the adult decorates the table, and the children help on the following days. The same story is told for a whole week. We tell old folktales or fables which are rich, not just through their vocabulary and linguistic style, but also through their imagery. We often use the stories as a means of communicating with a child who may be having problems of some kind. It is important that the adults engage in their own work in interpreting the tales, because this gives us a vehicle to reach the children. The story-teller learns it by heart and tells the tale without dramatizing it so that each child has an opportunity to create his own images based on his own developmental stage. We are careful not to let the youngest children participate in story-telling. If it is a long story, the three-year-olds sit in another room and draw, because in my experience it is important not to engage them in activities for which they are not ready. The exception to the rule at our center is birthdays, in which everybody participates.

When we have finished the story, the older children between five and seven years old are sent out to play. They have a special cloakroom over in my house, and put on their coats and jackets together with an adult. They spend about half an hour playing in the front yard on their own, before the rest of the children join them. This younger group needs more time to get its clothes on and the children do it themselves, with just a little help. We give them the opportunity to take their time.

Around 1:30, we gather around the garden table for a snack. It is usually a sandwich and an apple or raisins. The toddlers are now out of bed (although the youngest may still be asleep). At 2 pm, the parents start arriving, and by 2:30 the children have all been picked up. The last thirty minutes sometimes seems like forever to a small child. Once the gate opens, the spell is broken, and the toddlers have had enough. They want to go home. The older children aren't quite as eager to leave.

Once the parents arrive, they only stay for a short while. They say hello, pick up the backpack and their children, and then it's goodbye. If there is something special to be shared, we let the parents know, but we try to avoid too much talk. The child is impatient: he has been picked up and it is time to go home. The parents may go to the shop and talk there, but the children have become the parents' responsibility as soon as they have left the center.

Parent Relations

It is sometimes difficult to determine how many meetings we need with the parents. We have four or five parent meetings for the entire center every year. In addition, there are four meetings for parents of children under three, a meeting for the four-year-olds, one for the five- and one for the six-year-olds. All spring there are bazaar evenings every fortnight, which may include speakers from other places.

We visit every child in his home when he starts at the center, and we may visit once or twice during his time at the center. We are always available for special situations. In a divorce situation, we may be invited to assist in assessing the child's need for access. The center is neutral ground; here we work with the child's needs. As a care giver, I am neutral towards the needs of the parents. I may contribute with my experience and my knowledge of the child, if required.

We have an Anthroposophical doctor attached to the center who may be consulted twice a year. If they wish, the parents may use this service. Dr. Abigaard checks the child in the presence of the parents. If they wish, I also participate. As a result, most children take Anthroposophic remedies which aim at improving their general health in the long term.

Seasonal Celebrations

Our center has ten seasonal events:

Easter

May Day

Pentecost

Summer - Goodbye to children starting school

Harvest

Michaelmas

Lantern festival

Advent Spiral

Christmas (Twelfth Night)

Shrove tide/Spring

Most of the celebrations are for the children over three. The younger children take part in the preparations, but often they don't participate in the actual event, as they are asleep or at home. It will be their turn once they grow a little older. It is difficult for them to cope with too many impressions when they are still so young. It is important and valuable, however, for the children to participate in and to recognize the preparations.

Celebrating the seasons represents an external way of showing appreciation of cosmic events. We don't tell this to the children, but it lives in the spiritual work of the adults. Without constant study and enlivenment on a spiritual level, I would not survive my work in child care. The fact that I must always strive to improve myself, transform and express my experience, makes my work interesting, opening up new possibilities and points at areas that need study.

The seasonal celebrations are like pearls on a string, one after the other. Every season has a start, a middle, and an ending. It is a movement, a gliding movement into the next season. We are very lucky to live in a country where the seasons are easy to distinguish. I have just been to New Zealand, where they celebrate Christmas in the middle of summer. Here you would need to celebrate in a different way. The birth of Christ is a cosmic event whether it is winter or summer on earth. The outer form would be different, but the content the same.

Birthdays

A child's birthday is celebrated on the actual day. A birth is a very individual event. If two children celebrate their birthday on the same date, we have two celebrations that day. In the morning when the child arrives, we sing a birthday song: "Guess what day it is today; today it's Cecilie's birthday, we will get chocolate cookies from the baker, and maybe there is a surprise for her, but we are not saying." Then we shake hands. We ask her about her morning: "Did you wake up very early this morning?" The child has brought an edible surprise for dessert (not sweets). In our morning song circle, we sing the birthday song again, and maybe the birthday girl or boy tells us something.

We return from our walk half an hour early to give us ample time for the story. Once all the children have taken off their outdoor things, we gather in the dining room on benches in a circle. Then we sing birthday songs in all the languages spoken by children in the center. We sing in English, German, Finnish, Swedish, Dutch, French, Norwegian, and then in Danish.

The birthday child now crawls over the bench to be the first to open the door to the fairy-tale room, where a special birthday story table has already been set with lots of silk, decorative stones, lots of candles, flowers, and elves. Behind the story table are two thrones, one for the birthday child and one for the storyteller. Around them are chairs and stools for all the visitors. Once everybody is in the room, the storyteller gets up and bids the visitors welcome. The candles are lit and all the elemental spirits are bid welcome. We invite undines, salamanders, elves, fairies, angels, sylphs, pixies, trolls, dwarves, and last, but not least, the gnomes. Then the storyteller sits down. The birthday child then puts on the golden crown from the story table and we all exclaim that this is indeed a true birthday child. Then the child puts on the birthday robe. It is made of red velvet with golden edges. It is the same robe every year because the important element is to see how far down the robe goes on the child and then to exclaim that yes, this is indeed a real four-year-old girl — just under the knee.

Because the youngest children are also participating, it is important that everything happens at a continuous pace and that they have something to look at or even do. This is why our birthday story includes movements, eurythmy movements of the arms suitable for the situation. Now the beeswax candles are

Nøkken

lit, because first Cecilie turned one, then two, then three, and today she is four years old.

A birthday story:

Once upon a time, more than four years ago, Cecilie wasn't here on earth at all. Oh no, Cecilie was up in heaven with her guardian angel. She had a lovely time. She could roll around, she could hop first on one leg and then on the other without falling even once.

Then one day her guardian angel came and gave her a ball of real gold. Cecilie played with her golden ball. She threw it high into the air and caught it again. She threw it from one hand to the other without dropping it at all.

Then one day, when she was in a really strange and peculiar sort of mood, she thought she would see how far she could throw the ball. She picked it up, felt its weight in her hand at her shoulder, aimed, and threw it as far as as she could. She threw it so far that the ball disappeared. She searched here, there and everywhere, but the ball was nowhere to be found. Then suddenly she saw something shine among the clouds. And lo and behold, there was the ball, and as she reached for the ball, her eyes caught sight of earth. There she saw a beautiful sight. She saw a mother who moved her body so beautifully, and who had hair so long it cascaded all the way down her back, and she saw a father who had made a cradle ready for a little baby.

"Oh look," said Cecilie to her guardian angel, "May I go and visit them?"

Nøkken and Its Environment

"Yes," the guardian angel said, "you may, but first we will go for a very long walk. Past the sun and the moon and all the stars, through the gates of heaven right through to the rainbow gate, where you take off your heavenly clothes. I will look after them until you return." Then the small child fell asleep.

The mother reached up her arms and carried the small child under her heart for many, many days and weeks and months, until one day there was a tiny girl in the cradle. She had the most beautiful blue eyes, a tiny nose, and a tiny mouth that smiled.

"Oh," said the father and the mother, "She is the greatest gift of all. We will name her Cecilie because that is the very best name for her."

Then comes a small story about the child's development. A small beeswax candle is lit and sent around the circle of children, who sing:

Joy and happiness for your birthday, light for your future.

We sing this again and again, until the candle has passed around the circle of children and reached the birthday child. Then a small bell is rung over the birthday present. The child takes the gift and unwraps it. The number of tissue-paper layers around the present corresponds to the child's age. The gift is determined by the age of the child.

Nøkken

One and two-year-olds are given a hand-sewn doll, three-year-olds, a doll with legs. The children get dolls in colors appropriate for them (blue, red, or yellow). A four-year-old gets a little woolen elf with his friend, a mouse. It is important to look after your friends or they will run away. This also applies to the mouse. A five-year-old gets a crystal, and a six-year-old a scout's knife that he or she may bring to the center from that day on. There are special rules for knife bearers. A seven-year-old gets an individual present.

Now it is time to jump into the new year, and after the jump, we all clap our hands.

Then it is time to eat. After lunch comes a special dessert, often a birthday cake which the birthday child's family has made, and then the birthday is over. The child has been the center of attention long enough, as long as the child can cope.

The child takes home the present and the rest of the candle, which is lit at the evening meal at home.

International Relations

It is important to see yourself as an educator and to understand the part you play at a higher level. All too often we lose sight of this in the practicalities of daily life. The most important gift we can give the children is to continue to develop ourselves. The first years of a child's life are the most important years, for this is when he develops his joy of life. So it is crucial that we offer the children the best conditions: adults who understand that development takes time, peace and quiet, loving, insightful care, and self-education. Through her relation to the joy of life, the educator's engagement in life enriches the child.

Two major international conferences are held each year where the development of the child is discussed from a spiritual view. This is an opportunity for Waldorf educators from all over the world to meet and discuss current issues. It is a very strong experience to meet 1,000 educators from all over the world who are also working with young children. In spite of language, religion, cultural, and material differences, we all want the same thing: to create a world for our children which allows the individual child to find her path in life.

Feeling the inspiration from far continents and hearing about the cultural and social relations in other countries certainly helps a Dane to stop looking inward and to understand that it is important to participate actively in the rest of the world; we are very privileged in our lives. At Nøkken we have adopted a child-care center in Rumania. We have acted as hosts for trainees from all over the world, in particular from Eastern Europe, and the parents have offered a bed, food, excursions, and simple hospitality. To be able to act, to do something visible, means that whatever you hear in the media becomes more relevant. We don't feel passive, for together we make a difference. It nurtures the children.

When we are together at international events and discuss child care, it becomes clear that children are the same all over the world, regardless of the social environment. A child's development in the first years follows a set pattern. This is particularly clear from their drawings. Children draw in the same way for their first five years, whether they are from Russia, China, or Europe. Children draw from their own physical, organic development (see the bibliography).

Funding

Nøkken receives a grant from the Copenhagen City Council, and the parents pay a fee. We are funded under a pool system, which means that we receive a set amount per child. The amount is smaller than that granted to child-care centers run by the Council. The parents pay the same amount. The council requires annual accounts audited by a chartered accountant.

We have our own waiting list (which is very long), but report all new entries and withdrawals to the central allocation service. We are allowed to take children from other suburbs if their local council offers the same funding. Some councils do not. It is very unsatisfactory that a child can get caught in a bureaucratic web because of one council's inflexible policy. As our children usually live nearby, it is not a major problem, but if the family moves, a problem may arise. If a child has moved, or perhaps even lost a parent, it is important that the child not have to change her child-care center. How do you make a politician or a bureaucrat understand this enough to initiate change?

Nøkken and Its Environment

Our budget is based on 26 children, with eight under the age of three. We have a staff of four; three are trained Waldorf educators, and one is a 30-hour assistant. We all receive pay with pension-plan contributions in accordance with the current award. We do not have an award agreement with BUPL (organization of child-care givers), as we feel that it would to some extent curtail our freedom. It is very difficult for trade unions to understand that we are actually our own employers and are comfortable with the situation. We regard the City Council as a partner, and we trust each other. The staff are all members of a trade union.

A major item on the budget is rent. We have just purchased one of the buildings, after having rented it for seven years. With help from Merkur, an Anthroposophic bank, we procured a loan which enabled us to take out a mortgage with a building society. Our rent will be the same as before, but in ten years the house will be ours. The money left after rent is used for other fixed items. If we have special wishes, we have to save. I believe that it is good for us to make a special effort to achieve something. Once we have achieved our goal, we take special care of it. Our tight economy does worry me, in particular in case of sickness or maternity leave. We then need to renegotiate with the City Council.

We have had a special needs care giver attached to the center, paid by the Council, and in this connection we work well together with the established system. We are not afraid of learning from experts; on the contrary, it gives an incredible boost to our work.

Nøkken

During the ten years I have worked with children, I have seen an increase in the number of children who have difficulties being quiet and concentrating. We also see an increase in the number of children with problems determined by our culture and environment, such as hyperactive children and "attention deficit disorder" children. These children have very high care requirements which are both resource and staff intensive. One way to accommodate their needs is for the children to attend only one center outside of their homes. The staff should be as constant as possible. Our center has a rhythm and peacefulness of its own, and it offers the children a chance to understand themselves and their daily life while at the same time offering a long-term care program. Completely normal children have the same requirements as children with special needs. As staff, we can learn a lot from difficult children, and sometimes the children also benefit from the exchange. Who is normal, after all? However, we are very aware of our limitations and do not have more than two care-intensive children in our group.

How do we create a good workplace? A good workplace has its basis in an inner understanding of the child's requirements and our own development, a workplace where you are directly responsible for whatever happens during the day. When we hire new staff at Nøkken, it is for at least one year at a time.

We have trainees from the Rudolf Steiner College and from other colleges (we are not able to offer any pay for trainees). We have many overseas trainees who wish to experience our child-care center.

Nøkken and Its Environment

We see our center as a place in constant change, with a daily rhythm based on experience, but with change and development at our side. Working with children is the most fruitful and challenging job I can imagine. Life with the children, their parents, and my colleagues challenges every side of me all the time. I can safely say that self-education and development are never boring.

Afterword

An Experience

I was washing the dishes and let my thoughts fly. Suddenly I left my body, I flew up (I was still washing up); I landed on the peak of a high mountain. A huge bird, like an eagle, flew up to me and challenged me to fly. "I can't," I answered in my thoughts. "Try," it insisted. I looked out over the horizon. Everything seemed far away, but incredibly beautiful and still. I lifted my arms and the wind took me. I was flying, first with the bird and then alone. I flew past mountains, through valleys; it was a wonderful feeling. The sun shone. Then I came to a valley which was extremely beautiful. I flew towards the ground. I could see some crops. At first they looked like cabbages, but then I could see them changing to flower buds, and as I flew closer, they turned towards me slowly and looked up at me. In the flower buds I could see small heads, children's heads, looking up at me and smiling intimately and openly. I flew over the field of smiling children's faces, and then suddenly I was standing at the sink again.

It was an incredible experience. I had no doubt that it had happened. I knew, too, what it meant: that even though there would be many difficulties in starting a day care center, there was no doubt it was the right thing to do — the demand was there. So, even though I might be called utopian, an idealist and other such emotionally charged terms, I decided I was going to try to meet this need. And anyway, aren't these qualities, together with all the many others we develop throughout our lives, that are the impetus to action?

Helle Heckmann

Helle Heckmann — a short biography.

Helle was born in Copenhagen in 1955. She studied geography at the University of Copenhagen, following which she took up work in that field. In 1987 she began her Waldorf teacher training in Copenhagen, after which she developed the work with the child from ages one to seven.

In addition to her work with the child-care center Nøkken, Helle is active in teacher training and mentoring around the world. She participates in the working circle "From Birth to Three." She has started slowparenting.dk to meet the needs of parents as well as care givers.

A Garden for Kids

A Celebration of Nøkken

NOTE TO THE 2015 EDITION: *A booklet gathering contributions from the teachers, parents, and friends of Nøkken was produced in 2003 in celebration of the center's sixteenth year. We have added selections from its contents to this new edition of* Nøkken, *in the hope that they will enrich readers' understanding of the daily life and work of this remarkable place.*

Can I Take Care of Other People's Children?
• HELLE HECKMANN

Being a parent is a 24-hour-a-day job. One can never lay that responsibility aside, night and day and for the rest of one's life. The question for me as a professional care provider is whether I can take care of other people's children.

Can I provide the individual consideration that each child requires? I don't want to replace the parents, but at the same time I want to be the one who creates a stable and caring everyday environment.

I know that I would not have been able to do that if I weren't myself a mother; I don't consider being a parent a prerequisite for others, but it is a necessity for me personally. Another necessity for me is the anthroposophical vision of humanity. It will always be meaningful to work with children, but just the fact of being able to go deeper into the spiritual development of people, considering my work as a part of my own self-education, gives a holistic aspect to my work life and my personal life. The fact that as a spiritually seeking person, I can go deeper into anthroposophy and through that process get an understanding for human development, the meaning and significance of the individual person, means that I can, in my limited way, meet the child, hold myself back, and let the child show the way along its own path. I must not make the children be as I wish. From my example, through my inner work that is mirrored in my action in the outside world, I must offer the children a meeting with an adult who takes life and the meeting with each person seriously. Through my insight about the child's needs, I must take responsibility for my actions and create a framework within which children can unfold in all security and comfort. Also, what we do in the kindergarten is not just what I want and feel like doing, but something I have consciously and thoroughly thought out with all my awareness before I initiate actions in the outer world.

A Celebration of Nøkken

I say yes to taking care of other people's children because I say yes to life and because I consider protecting childhood the most important thing in life, since it never comes again.

There will be no reruns of childhood! Childhood is the only chance a human being has to learn to step into the social environment. If that is taken from a person, we have missed our goal: love of our fellow human beings. Without that, there is no humanity.

The kindergarten Nøkken started in 1987 as a day care center for children from birth to three years of age, located in my own home in Copenhagen, Denmark. The youngest child, my own, was two months old. There were also two six-month-old children, one one-year-old, and one two-year-old. The opening times were from 8:30 am to 2:30 pm.

In Denmark, about 80 percent of the children over one year of age are taken care of by other people than their parents. Before children reach kindergarten age, they have most often been exposed to up to four different child care options including private child care, communal day care centers, nurseries, and groups of small children. It means that before children enter kindergarten they have experienced many shifts during the most important years of life, and has been exposed to the care of several adults, as well as to unknown numbers of other children. The most vulnerable time in a person's life has been the most full of turbulence. Kindergarten and school are planned and structured, but the first years might as well be gotten over as quickly as possible.

In Denmark, it is quite natural for children under three years of age to have constantly running noses, and to be not ill but not well either. They have the highest attendance rate in institutions and their parents are those who work the most. Divorce rates are very high. It brings about a family structure where the child is split between several homes.

For all these reasons, I wanted to create a place, a home for children, not an institution. A place where children feel comfortable, where they are in contact with the same adults all the time (no alternating shifts), where daily life is built around an understanding of the child's needs.

After a year, the two-year-old had become a three-year-old and should have gone on to kindergarten. But I found that wrong. He should be with me, and so I had to set up a place for children of all ages until school age, where the older children could learn empathy towards the younger ones and the younger children could look up to the older ones—in other words, a place where children could learn from one another. This way siblings could remain together, while only children could learn to take care of younger children and show consideration for others than themselves.

A Garden for Kids

That is why Nøkken is now a place for children in ages ranging from those starting to walk to grade school age. As an educator, it is a wide spectrum to span, but it is also a delightful challenge. We have presently 24 to 26 children, about three to four in each year of age. This offers the possibility to play with younger or older children, depending on where each child is in its own development. Typically, the three- to four-year-olds remain very young for a time before they take a big step into the world of fantasy and social life. There is room for that because our rhythm is adapted to all ages.

They don't have to grow up fast.

After our first year, I found that taking care of children who cannot walk was simply too demanding to allow their integration in a large group. The many meals, the more numerous nap times, the need for care and peace and quiet, as well as close contact with adults, made it too difficult. The several physical developmental steps—rolling, crawling, sitting up, trying to walk—all require a lot of quiet and comfort, which is difficult to find in a large group. And we could not meet that need in a responsible manner.

The composition of daily life is well thought out, depending on the kind of children we have. We are located in a large city. Most children live in apartments. As already mentioned, many families are split, and many don't have social networks. For these reasons, we take mainly children from the local area so that they can see one another outside kindergarten times. This way, the parents can also assist one another taking care of the children and have some social life together.

We value physical development very much. Nowadays, there are serious problems due to reduced physical activity because children don't get to move as much as they could or should.

Every day, rain or shine, we all take walks. The children need to move. If we were to just stay in our wonderful garden some of the children would just sit. Movement gives joy to life. The child learns to know its body's abilities, and develops self-confidence. Language comes with movement, which is why we don't have dedicated singing in a circle. We sing when we walk, with great joy! If the wind blows we sing wind songs, seasonal songs, and so on.

Moving is fun. It stimulates the appetite and results in healthy tiredness.

We go to specific places, large parks where the walks take about twenty minutes. We stay there and the children can play freely on the grass, in the trees, and around the bushes. We adults bring along needlework, hand weaving, spindles, carving knives, clothes that need mending. We are located at specific places so that the children know where we are. They can thus play in great confidence that they know where to go should the need arise. We try not to interfere too much with their activities. We also limit surveillance and constant comments about the children's behavior.

Of course, there are rules of behavior. The children may fight, but not bite, hit others on the head or face, pinch or scratch, etc. When a child says "No thanks," it means stop, and it must be respected.

We can see clearly that children between one and two years of age, and some of the three-year-olds too, observe their environment and participate a little, but clearly stick to some adults whom they use as the center of their activities. The older they get the further they venture from that center. The big children are out and up in the trees, totally taken by play.

A Celebration of Nøkken

Play is the fundamental ingredient in our kindergarten. Playing is the jumping-off point for social life. Here all the dramas that are necessary to become a human being can unfold themselves. Both the beautiful and ugly sides are being tried out here, which deepens the understanding that there are other people in life, and that to be together with others one must show consideration. It is important to listen to others than oneself. This has surely become a central issue in today's kindergartens.

We come back home around 10:30 and we are very hungry by the time we get home around 11. The group is then split: there are eight one-to-two year-olds who are taken care of by two adults and sometimes a student. They have a little wooden house in the back of the kindergarten. They change clothes in peace and quiet and eating is highly concentrated work. The bigger children, three to seven, eat in the bigger wooden house, where there is a livelier ambiance. The children learn about table manners, about which many know little.

We make very simple food at the kindergarten, from biodynamic products: rice on Mondays, oats on Tuesday, millet on Wednesday, all simply boiled in water. On Thursdays we have vegetable paté and seasonal vegetable soup on Fridays. We consider that common eating is an important social gathering opportunity. All eat with great appetite.

After eating the younger children take a nap until about 1:30 pm. The older children hear a story. The five-to-seven-year-olds go out so that there can be fewer children in the garden, with an adult who chops wood, saws, carves, does some gardening, etc. The three-to-four-year-olds are now inside for half an hour while an adult is cleaning up, decorating windows, or preparing for seasonal festivals. The children play with dolls, dress up, or rest on the couch.

After that, they go to the changing room where it takes a long time for them to put their coats on. They then play in the garden until a group snack around 1:30 pm and pick-up time between 2 and 2:30 pm. The children are tired but glad, and there is still the chance for spending a little time with the parents before dinner and bedtime. The children are still their parents' children.

The work of the adults at the kindergarten is very practical, with three old houses and a garden of about 900 square meters, many apple trees, gardening beds, chickens, rabbits, without mentioning warming with wood stoves, all of which requires an incredible amount of work for daily life to function adequately. Consequently, the basis for our pedagogical work is imitation, a quite natural part of daily life.

The children can play side by side with an adult who is taken by his or her own work. The adult engages in meaningful work that the child takes in. The mere experience of how life's basic fundamentals happen strengthens the child's own development and understanding of how things hang together. This happens through doing.

It is a sizeable task for us educators to relate to our kindergartens in a new way. Because children spend more time in institutions than at home, this influence has a significant meaning for the children. When the children are home, they often go to other places: to visit people, to the gym, etc. The parents' need to do their best to activate and stimulate the child brings about an incredible level of stress for the adult. Home values lose priority. In the many split families where the child lives between two homes, with new "fathers," new "mothers" and new "siblings" and the like, the kindergarten provides a new aspect; it becomes the stable home. Are our kindergartens ready for this?

It must be said that all parents work and Nøkken's opening hours make it difficult for them. They have had to obtain reduced working hours, as well as more consideration for family life. They have deliberately chosen another way of life with a reduction of pace and a lower standard of living. This requires a definite conscious choice.

It is important for me to assist parents as they recover the meaning of the family. If parents and children don't get a close-knit relationship during childhood, what will happen later in life, from youth to old age?

When people ask me what is most difficult about working in a kindergarten, I must necessarily answer: the work on myself to meet others. Meeting the children is very uncomplicated, if I have done my homework well. I need to be well prepared for the daily tasks, as well as with talks, songs, the daily routine, and reflections on the previous day.

Meeting parents and especially colleagues is considerably more complicated. It is a big issue for me to find out how we, individualists as we are, can want to meet, and through listening to each other, create a common vision of our relationships so that we can create an enlivened existence together.

I am willing, but very often it feels like taking two steps back for each step forward. To believe that Steiner/Waldorf kindergartens are small, isolated paradise islands where children don't meet life's harsh sides is an illusion. The adult's shortcomings ensure that this doesn't happen.

I love my work and I will continue to believe that it is the most meaningful job in the world.

One Week in the Life of Nøkken

• TIRIL, INTERN AT NØKKEN

I did my internship in a kindergarten called Nøkken in Copenhagen. It is located right in the middle of the city, and yet it feels as if it is in the countryside. There are three teachers at Nøkken. Helle Heckmann, who started the kindergarten fifteen years ago, is the daily leader. She takes care of the smallest children in Lille Nøkken (Small Nøkken). Soren is primarily with the middle group, and Rune has the older children, but the middle and older groups are mixed together. Liv is an assistant teacher working part-time. I suspect that Liv hides a magic wand somewhere, simply because she can really do magic. She can turn a sad, gray basement into a convivial dining room with light, warmth, and a delightful, quiet harvest atmosphere. Otherwise, she is with the smaller children. There are three interns, Daniella, a first-year intern, Tove, a third-year intern, and myself. Altogether, there are twenty-seven children at Nøkken with nine in each age group.

Monday

I ride my bicycle in the rain on my way to Nøkken. The streetlights will soon be turned off, and it won't be long until the church bells ring. It is almost 8:00 am. I make my way down Stovnes Allé, looking for Nøkken. I come to a large, comfortable, yellow house with climbing roses on each side of the door. There is also another brand new house next door. I can almost smell the Swedish fir of which it is built. The area around the house is a construction site. The house patiently waits to start its function as the "New" Nøkken. I cross the gate that stands between the two houses, and I enter Nøkken's garden. There is a vague cover of fog and chimney smoke. Daniella has started the wood stove in Lille Nøkken. I am met with an open hand and a smile, "Good morning." We welcome each other and a new day. The church bells ring and we start our morning meeting, standing outside as we always do. There we read relevant literature, talk about the day, and mention which children are not coming. The verses for the day and the week are read aloud with devotion. In that morning time, stillness and a force are being planted in me as a small seed.

It is 8:30 am, and the day has begun. The children slowly start streaming in through the gate. Each of us starts doing some meaningful work. Helle and Daniella hang laundry to dry near Lille Nøkken. Tove gives some fresh hay to the rabbits while Rune and I are in full swing sawing wood. A six-year-old boy standing near Soren greets us, "Good morning." He comes directly towards us with outstretched arms. "Good morning, Peter. Good morning, Tiril." He is anticipating with joy a new and eventful day in the kindergarten. The garden is now nearly full of children, and it is close to 9:00 am. Helle calls out for the children to come to the morning circle by singing: "All the children must come now, we are going to sing!" The circle is formed and a beautiful seasonal song resonates. Helle continues with, "Good morning altogether, a new day starts. Jonas is here, Sine is here, Helle is here." When our name is called out, we bow to show that we are present. We are now here all together. Above the clouds the sun shines, round and golden. All the children greet each other first on one side and then on the other, and each and every flower and every bird. The firs and the birches whistle in the fresh

A Garden for Kids

wind. Hear all the roosters that stand and crow in the morning, Cock-a-doodle-doo!

Helle says, "Will you please hop on one leg to the gate." Small and large, we all hop out through the gate, on our walk to the roundabout. A three-year-old boy goes with me, hand in hand. He is tired so we don't say anything. We walk and listen to Tove's beautiful lantern song: "Lantern, lantern, sun, moon and stars. Shine my light high, shine my light high." Rune goes first, and all the children follow him in a long line. My place is in the middle between Rune and the youngest who come at the end with the carriages, or in them. It is Helle or Daniella who push the carriages. I must make sure that all the older children walk in front of the carriages.

We stop just after coming through the cemetery gate, for that is the area we call the roundabout. Here, there is a lot of room to play freely among many kinds of trees. There are trees to climb and bushes to hide and make caves in. There is room to play for all. A four-year-old girl and boy are used to having a specific tree, a slanted fir that is grouped with other trees, forming a corner by the roots. Here they climb to the top, sitting and chatting until it is time for the singing game. In the middle of the roundabout stands a huge tree, its trunk stable and strong with its lowest branches high up. This is where Helle and the youngest children are, for it is a good and safe place.

Rune takes his stick and knife out and walks around quietly, keeping a discreet eye on what is going on in the corners. Tove has found her hand-spinning tool and her wool box while Soren carves a beet into a lantern. All are well spread around the whole area. I look for a good piece of wood that could possibly become a small mouse. While I look around, I have good opportunities to take a peek into the different games the children play. The sun breaks through between the trees, but the cold bites our cheeks a bit. It is about 10:00 am when Rune calls the children to come to him for the singing game. After that, the children play freely again until 10:30 am.

A little boy's stomach starts to rumble. We know it because he begins to call out as Helle does when is time to go home, "All children must come now, we must go home!" The children stream from the corners to the place where we gather before going home. Today we have rice pudding on the menu. After the meal, Tove tells a fairy tale. She does it for two weeks and then it will be Soren's turn.

The atmosphere from the fairy tale remains during the playtime in the garden that follows. There is no shortage of creativity or fantasy. The children play freely in the garden before and after snack at 1:30 pm. In the meantime, I paint the swing chair. When it gets to be 2:15 pm. it is time to clean up. The parents start to come to pick up their children. The last ones come to the waiting stair. We shake hands, "Goodbye, thank you for today."

After all of the children are gone, the adults form a circle and take each other's hand. If we have any comments regarding the day that just finished, then we share them at this time. Then we say, "Goodbye and thank you for today."

Tuesday

It is 8:30 am, and a six-year-old girl comes through the gate. She greets us all, and we greet her, "Good morning!" The garden becomes more and more lively as children fill it. After the morning song, we must walk backwards towards the gate! It is fun to see how good the children are at it—they don't fall at all! When we reach the street and all are gathered, Rune watches carefully for cars and bicycles before standing in the middle of the street with his arms stretched out: "Will you now cross the street?" Two four-year-old girls are not thinking about going anywhere today; they stand to look at something on the ground, and could have discussed what it was for ten minutes. But we must move along. "On your way, on your way!" They know that well, and get going at a good pace.

We reach the roundabout. Because of the light rain, we have taken rain clothes with us, and the hats are tight. None of that gets in the way of the playing. It is nice to be here, rain or shine. Today, some boys have an interesting experience. A four-year-old boy jumps from the lowest branch of a large tree. He is sure of his jump, but a small branch gets caught in his coat. He is stuck in a position that is not dangerous for him. Then I see two other boys, one six and the other four, come to help him, so I choose to let them try to manage it on their own. The bigger and stronger six-year-old boy starts lifting the hanging child while the four-year-old concentrates on freeing the coat from the branch. They do not manage at the first attempt, but that is no reason for giving up! By the third time, the boy in the tree begins to get tired of hanging there and starts mumbling something to the others to the effect of getting an adult to help. Helle also follows what is going on and says in a loud voice that I can go and help. But as soon as the boys hear that, they put all their energy into that last attempt that had to succeed, and it does! I have seldom seen two boys be so proud of themselves. It highlights for me that the experience of being able to do something by oneself strengthens self-esteem and the desire to try.

After the singing game, two of the older boys think that there is not enough happening, and they start putting dirt into the drinking water bottle. They find it very enjoyable until Tove catches them in the act. Tove is strict, for she did not find their prank very amusing. They consequently have to sit for a time by Helle. The conniving, mischievous looks slowly fade from their faces as more and more of the other children come to have a drink. The boys realize that it was not really funny that the others should be thirsty because they put dirt in the drinking water. I believe that it will be a while before those boys do that type of action again.

"All children must come now, we must go home!" It is 10:40 am, and stomachs rumble. We gather and start to walk back home. When we reach the gate, the youngest go to Lille Nøkken, while the middle and older group go down to the basement cloakroom. When eighteen children come into such a small room, the temperature rises quickly, and the temptation to make trouble grows. It is as if the air gets overfilled with energy. Soren starts singing the Lantern Song, and the children concentrate on taking off their coats.

One four-year-old boy could sit on the floor forever. It looks like he is building castles in the air on those four buttons sewn to his coat. I ask him to take his boots off. He looks at me and kindly asks for help. But Soren says that he can manage by himself. He does finally manage, but he needed the extra time. The older children are quickly done taking off their coats and washing their dirty hands in warm water. They are really quite good at helping the smaller ones: pulling tight boots off and untying scarves.

We go into the most central room in the basement. Earlier this morning, when I looked in, it was full of painting supplies and seemed a bit sad. But Liv had been there in the meantime with her magic wand: she had made a partition with a piece of cloth so the painting supplies were hidden, and she had decorated the place with candles and tablecloths.

When all are sitting at their places, Rune

A Garden for Kids

asks for quiet. There are three candles on the table, surrounded by autumn leaves. Rune strikes a match and lights the candles, letting one child blow out the match. Rune sits down, and we sing our blessing. Rune asks a six-year-old boy to be his helper today. The boy is glad to do so and starts dishing out the rice pudding with a serious look on his face. To preserve the quiet, Rune tells a little story about the time he broke his arm when he was a child. In the meantime, I pour warm herb tea in glasses and cups. The children are hungry, and they eat the food as soon as they get it.

While we eat, Soren and Rune often tell small stories, which helps the children eat and be quiet instead of fooling around with each other. Consequently, the noise is considerably less. A little three-year-old boy manages to eat four servings before he has had enough. While I clean up later on, I can see that others have secretly dropped a couple of bites on the floor. The children use the bathroom and get ready to go outside for a story and playtime.

When I am done cleaning up, I go out to the garden. Fairy tale time is already over, and the children are quite involved with playing. I find a mess of leaves, old bricks and rotting apples in the back of the playhouse. I clean up there until snack time. Two small boys, almost three years old, saying they will be glad to help me clean away leaves and apples, come with a small wheelbarrow and a shovel. They can't talk very well yet, so we sing songs. We eat our snack, and yet another day is almost gone.

I greet the father of my two helpers and say: "Good-bye and thank you for today."

Wednesday

We sing and shout: "Cock-a-doodle-doo!" We shout especially loud today because Helle had told us that Mohammed, one of the carpenters, had not heard us at all yesterday. "You must go to the gate on stiff legs!" Rune takes us safely across the street, and we joyfully get going, but today, we are not going to the roundabout. Instead, we go to the rolling slope. The rolling slope could at first glance look like the roundabout: tall trees with long and heavy branches reaching all the way down to the ground; bushes and scrubs to hide. But here there are stone stairs and a large grass area. There is another atmosphere, too. The trees are closer together here, which makes it a bit more secretive than the roundabout. The older children rejoice over the possibility of having a large hiding place without adults, and if an adult should come by, the voices go to whispers and murmurs. It is nice to have something that is your own.

I sit, carving my stick, when I suddenly notice three children up in a tree. They are well underway towards an argument with loud voices. Two boys (four and five) and a four-year-old girl, all three very energetic children, want to be the one to sit at the top of the tree. The voices get louder, and they are very close to getting really mad at one other. Helle breaks in and says that she does not want to have screaming children in trees, and if they are going to shout, they should come down from the tree. There is some mumbling up there in the tree, and after a short time, all three are sitting on the very same branch with a generous view over the grass area. There is room for all, and enough to talk about.

Over by the hedge is Helle's place, and the younger children putter around her. Diagonal from the hedge is the reason for the location's name, namely the rolling slope. Here they roll down the small slanted slope, on and off from time to time when they want to get a bit dizzy. It is almost 10 am and Rune calls the children

A Celebration of Nøkken

for the singing game. The smaller children may join in if they want to, and they often do. Rune gets down on his knees, and we gather in a circle. Two two-year-old boys are too fascinated by Rune's movements to follow him. Sometimes one hand comes up with a small motion that is slightly like Rune's, but they mostly sit with gaping mouths and are totally engrossed in what is going on. It is wonderful to watch children's intense desire to learn.

Rune stands up, and we all agree that it is a bit too cold to remain sitting on the ground. To get warmed up, Rune sings while he hops around a little: "Freezing, shivering, sneezing noses. Stamping, trampling, ouch the wind bites." The children laugh; it is so much fun to get warm that way. After the singing games, the children may play freely again until 10:30 am when it is time to go back.

We gather in front of the rolling slope and go home a different way than we usually do. On our way, we stop by each watering place and look. If it is freezing weather; we look to see if there is ice in the barrels. Fingers get cold from holding ice, but it is so fascinating that the children cannot resist playing with it.

After we come back home and fingers are warmed in the sink full of water with a few drops of Arnica oil, it is time to eat. We eat millet porridge today, with a bit of oil and warm tea that warms everyone up. It fills tummies very well. Soon all have their outdoor clothes on again and go out for the fairy tale.

Near Lille Nøkken, there is a small sandbox with a bit of grass around it. Carpets hang on the clotheslines to create an undisturbed space. This is the fairy tale room. Here each child can live in a world full of pictures—their own pictures of the story, which belong only to each individually.

One of the older children is the helper and sits next to Tove. The helper has a lyre on her or his lap. We have formed a circle in the middle of which there is a tree stump covered with silk, where a small lantern stands. Tove lights the lantern and sings for the fairy tale to come to her: "Fairy tale, fairy tale, come to me, I'd like to hear you." After that, the helper must play the lyre to make the fairy tale come down from the stars. Two fingers glide over each and every string. The same fairy tale is told all week. One must know it by heart, because after a couple of days, the children remember precisely how it was told, and one gets corrected if any words are forgotten. The story ends as it should, with everlasting happiness after hard challenges. Then the helper plays again to send the fairy tale back to the stars.

It is almost 1:30, and the children have played well in the garden. I have sawed enough wood for the stove for a couple of days, but there can never be too much firewood. All the children now come; for it is time for snack. We sing: "Ding, ding-a-ling, each takes a thing, cleaning up and laying down, all children must come along." After we clean the garden together, the children that have not

A Garden for Kids

been picked up by parents yet go to the waiting stair. The waiting stair has exactly six steps. The older children sit on the upper step, and soon down the steps by age, and wait until mother or father comes through the gate to get them. We greet the parents and say: "Good-bye and thank you for today."

Thursday

We welcome the children that have just arrived. A five-year-old boy has a tough time saying goodbye to his mother today. He cries and asks for his mother. His little brother looks at him with soft eyes. It is strange that his brother's crying does not rub off on him. After the morning song, the boy has overcome his difficult good-bye with his mother. He has his eyes on the new day and the upcoming experiences with his friends.

Before leaving for the roundabout, we try to walk to the gate on the tips of our toes. It is difficult with big boots, but all try the best they can, and if some cannot, they try to go backwards instead. It is funny to see how much they try to show what they can do rather than giving up. On the way to the roundabout, the lantern songs resonate. The songs sink into the children as the celebration gets nearer, and they talk with one another about the upcoming festival.

We arrive at the roundabout. There is a huge tree with long branches that hang low. It is perfect to climb, for the branches are supple. Those who have not yet figured out how to climb can simply hang and swing on the lowest branches. Two two-year-old boys have practiced climbing

in trees several times. They climbed up beautifully, but when it was time to come down, they regretted having climbed up so high. Somebody had to help them down. For that reason, they are not allowed to climb up in the big trees anymore. They stand and peep at the nice climbing trees. One day, they will dare to climb again. I'd like to see that day.

Rune does the singing game when it is about 10 am. The older children have whispered that they would like to hide from Rune during the singing game. Strangely enough, they are the first ones to show up when Rune calls out. Then, the children play freely for half an hour more until Helle calls them, and we are on our way back home again.

Today we shall eat paté. It tastes good, and the dish is soon empty. The cloakroom fills with children and songs; the energy is irreproachable. The older children are good at helping the younger ones with dressing. They know precisely what clothes belong to whom.

After the fairy tale, I get my small paint bucket and my paintbrush. Painting the swinging chair is a long process. The swinging chair stands in a corner of the garden, right next to the large sandbox. I hope that no one pays notice to my "wandering" ears. I have also a perfect view over the activities that go on in the garden. The children have been watching the carpenters build the new house long enough to know how it is done. They have been inspired, and the girls have stacked up some walls with pallets to make a room. They have added a board, some chairs and, at times, a computer. While they potter around and have a good time in their new house, a boy is well underway mixing cement. The water and sand is thoroughly mixed with a stick before it gets slapped on bricks, and nicely spread on top before a new brick is added. That, I must say, is the best and most clear example of imitation I have seen. In the end, it becomes a very nice house to decorate the garden.

While that goes on, some three-year-old children, two girls and a boy, come to me as I paint the swinging chair. Earlier, I had sung a song about a troll from the Norwegian forest that they wanted to hear again. Because I sing it in Norwegian, they pay close attention to understand what it is about (Danish and Norwegian are closely related languages). I keep painting while I sing, and it is not long before they paint with me with imaginary paint brushes, while their heads swing from side to side in pace with the song. In the garden, the older children help by cutting vegetables for tomorrow's soup. They sit and complain a bit about this "boring" task, but in fact they seem to enjoy the company. It is, in fact, quite a social activity to sit across from one another and prepare a common meal.

It is 1:30, and time to have a snack. The middle and older groups sit at the two long tables that stand in the garden. Rune comes with a basket full of appetizing apples. Each child gets one. "Oh, no! There is a worm in my apple," announces a four-year-old boy. "You should not worry about it," says a six-year-old girl. "It tastes just the same as the rest of the apple, and it is not dangerous." "Yeah," says the boy. He takes a puzzled look at his apple and eats the whole thing, quite satisfied with the wormy apple's taste. After they eat their apple, the children run out and play again.

The smallest children are also done eating their snack and a couple of two-year-old girls play well. One of them has tucked the other into a metal bucket, and she has a large blue sheet as a blanket. She gives the "baby" plenty of food and drink, too. (Here in the kindergarten, you are properly cared for.)

A Garden for Kids

Friday

Friday is a bit of a special day, because the younger children don't come to Nøkken. Consequently, this day offers different possibilities. When the children have arrived and we sing the morning song, it is not to the cemetery that we go, but to the swamp. The swamp is just down the street from the kindergarten. We follow the narrow path along the water. There are benches every twenty-five to thirty meters. The children may run and go freely, as long as they go forward, from bench to bench. When we are all gathered by the next bench, Rune says: "You may go on." Many interesting things can be found on the bank. These days, there is a dirt heap along the edge of the water, where the children find some large living mussels. They may also go down to the edge of the water, but they must then lie on their stomachs so that there is no risk of falling in. There is of course an adult along with a watchful eye.

We arrive at the large fallen willow tree, where we stay for a while. It is a good climbing tree and is also a charming tree, just waiting there for children to come and make it useful! A young swan comes out of the water to greet us, and we go to a clearing in the trees just across from the willow tree. There is a large fire pit with large stones. There is an outer circle of stones to sit on or to be used for a huge bonfire. Rune has brought some nice dry wood from the kindergarten, and he lights a little bonfire for us. At first, there are not so many children around the bonfire; they play on the large tree trunks next to it. Rune and I sit and carve a little, in the warmth from the bonfire.

One of the older children comes over and pulls his knife out; he wants to join the quiet. We do not say much to one another – we just carve. More come over, and we end up sitting all together. The smaller children use two wood sticks: one is a knife, and the other, well, a wooden stick. There is a relaxed and comfortable atmosphere. The eyes of some of us disappear in a dream into the flames of the bonfire, listening to Rune's story about his travels.

We put out the bonfire and head home. We have a little more time today, because there are no small children that must nap, and the soup that awaits us is better from sitting a bit. It takes a bit longer to get home because we walk another way. It takes us to the cemetery past a small artificial dam. There are bamboo bushes with narrow paths in them. I go in, and feel like a giant in a maze. Later, we go by a large stone that has been cut and polished in the water, with stairs to climb. It sways a little and makes rings in the water. The children who can manage on the stairs on their own may go on it. Those who cannot manage stand and watch—a foot is hesitantly placed on the first step, but goes no further. One day they will dare to take the first step.

We go on through the cemetery and up through the gate. By now, hunger starts gnawing, and the soup back home must be ready. Hands are washed, and we sit at the table. Rune lights the three candles on the table, and we say our blessing. The soup is dished out by one of the helpers, one of the oldest children, because the soup is very warm. It takes concentration not to spill any. We have water to drink instead of tea because we are eating warm soup.

When we are done eating it is fairy tale time. The fairy tale is told, goes back to the stars, and it is time again for free play until snack time. The workshop area in the garden is being well used. There is always somebody with a hammer or a saw. Only imagination can limit what two pieces of wood joined with a nail can become. It is a work of art created by one's own hand, and the joy is almost everlasting.

Again, it is time to clean up and go home. Both parents and children join hands and say: "Good-bye and thank you for today." We stand by the gate, gathered in a circle. For all of us, the week has been enriching and eventful. We are now exhausted and ready for the weekend. —*Translated by Jean-Paul Bardou*

Working with the Will
• RUNE BRATLANN, EDUCATOR

In Nøkken, we work with children as beings of will. Manual work, singing, unspoiled experience of the change in the seasons, tired feet and ravenous appetite, the smell of good food, are all elements that make a direct appeal to the will-power of the little child, which here is allowed to develop freely and in safe and recognizable surroundings. Although every day is different from the others, the rhythmical repetition and the organization of the day is the spine of the whole kindergarten.

The staff meets about one hour before the kindergarten opens, around 7:30. After that, the food is prepared and set to cook; the tables are set, the fairy tale room is prepared; the strollers are made ready and packed with blankets, water bottles, diapers, toilet paper; the pail with butter-knives, which the smallest children use to "whittle" with, plus all the different things we use in the preparation of our annual celebrations.

The little red cabin is the home of the youngest group of children, from one to three years of age. Here the cribs are made ready in the very best way, and the oven, which is in use from early fall to mid-spring, is lighted, with the smell of authentic comfort as a result. This is where we begin our indispensable morning reading at 8:00 sharp, even though everybody is not in the circle, because this way no one slows the morning down for everyone else, if he or she is not able to let go of a task. We start out by reading a selected text by Rudolf Steiner for about fifteen minutes, and within this period everybody in the circle is reading aloud from the text. Then follows the current verse from Rudolf Steiner's soul calendar, which helps us to weave ourselves into the day in the best possible way. After this, we go over the coming day in its more technical/practical aspects: who is sick, who needs extra care, who of the staff does what, and so on. Finally, we wish each other a fine day in the circle. Everybody knows what to do, the time is 8:30, and the first children and their parents are already waiting outside the gate.

Every day, the children and their parents are met with a warm handshake, after which the parents, quickly and without too much talking, disappear. The children then occupy the large and magnificent playground. They share it with the white Angora rabbit—which is often used as a transition from mother or father to a new day in the kindergarten for the youngest

A Garden for Kids

children. There are also our chickens, who, besides giving us their eggs, also work as a guarantee for all of our leftovers to be used, which is totally in agreement with the ecological spirit of the location, where nothing, even the dishwater, should be wasted. Instead, it must be integrated in a healthy, continuous consciousness of how everything is connected, lived out in a warm loving practice.

The children and adults gather in a circle at 9:00, and with a song, we welcome each other. We then walk for about twenty minutes, by routes we know like the back of our own hands. We stop for just over one hour at our usual playground—a big field with old trees and many excellent hideaways. There, the children can play by themselves in the beautiful surroundings while the adults work to prepare the next annual celebration, collect garbage from the area, build small twig-houses for the hedgehogs or whittle small wood figures.

When we come back home, we are all hungry. After we have taken off our outdoor clothes, changed from outdoor shoes to slippers, been to the toilet and washed our hands, the good food, which is always prepared in the most simple way and out of the finest biodynamic raw materials, is consumed with great appetite. We sing before and after the meal, and when we are finished, we all help each

other to clean up the table, so the whole kindergarten can sit there and paint, while the adults and a couple of helpers do the dishes and sweep the floors.

After some time, the fairy tale is ready, and the children can now enter the little and very cozy fairy tale room. After taking a deep breath, we are all looking forward to come out into the garden, where the children can play by themselves until 1:30, when fruit and water is served at the tables in the garden. After that, the adults begin to clean up the garden, normally assisted by some small helpers, the parents start to show up, and then the kindergarten closes for the day.

All day long there are things to be done—necessary and meaningful work that must be done in order to make life fit together. The children experience the working process from start to finish and can easily relate to what is going on, without words and admonitory speech, but rather full of joy in life itself.

The more conscious we adults become, the better we can ask ourselves this question over and over again: Why do I do what I do the way I do it? Thus it will become easier to enter the absolutely intimate, close, and practical reality that surrounds the children and defines their beings. Here it is of great importance that we endeavor to be present. Even in the smallest of our movements, we must fill out our body with consciousness in such a way that we—in the most literal understanding of the word—learn to stand up for what we are. To attain this goal, I cannot think of any better way than to be with young children. Nothing else can motivate that sacrifice it some times can be to get rid of all our little uglinesses, to grow out over the borders of our own (imaginary) limits, and to strive to become that truly happy and healthy human, worthy of imitation as an ideal, that the children need so deeply.

What I Remember from My Time at Nøkken
• HELENA REUMERT GJERDING,
 TWELFTH GRADER AT THE WALDORF SCHOOL

I will try to tell a bit about what it has been like to be in Nøkken and what it meant for me to attend a Waldorf kindergarten.

I have discovered that this is a difficult task, as I don't know what it would have been like to be in another kindergarten; I haven't got anything to compare with. But I know that I have a lot of good memories from my time in the kindergarten. I remember that we used our imaginations a lot, when we were out walking for example. We could spend hours preparing what we were going to play when we got back. I also remember how happy we were when we got a new playhouse in the kindergarten, but I don't recall ever using it for anything other than a hiding place. After all, who wants to live in a tiny house, when you can have a kitchen in the sandpit and a living room under the plum tree?

The fairy tales have also made a big impression on me. I clearly remember how cozy it was to sit in the small house and listen to the stories while the youngest children were asleep. I can still recall the atmosphere when it smells of burned matches.

Easter is also a time I remember well. How we tied flowers around eggs and boiled them in onion shells. They were so beautiful that my parents weren't allowed to throw them out before the whole living room smelled of rotten eggs. And even though I have never liked the taste of egg, and most definitely not of the yolk, there was something very special about this little yellow-green sun that appeared after I had thrown the egg seven or eight times. That made me eat it.

But what I remember most of all is the Wishing Tree and that very special feeling when you know that something isn't real and still believe in it. Even after I had left the kindergarten, I still used it every time I came by, and it was a very sad day when I discovered that somebody had chopped down half of it.

Maybe I can't say specifically what I have got out of being in Nøkken, and maybe the events didn't happen exactly as I recall them, but that doesn't really matter. What matters is that I have had some great experiences that I can always look back on and remember the special feelings that were connected with them.

The Course of Life

• HELLE HECKMANN

I often ask myself the question: "What is it that makes me call my kindergarten a Rudolf Steiner kindergarten?"

On the inside, it is my own search and my working out of Rudolf Steiner's ideas, as well as working on the spiritual image of humanity. But this is a process that takes place constantly in me, where I am now. It has nothing to do with the surroundings—and yet, the interaction with the surroundings is in itself the education process, for without interaction the individuality is in and of itself pointless.

But what do these thoughts have to do with working with children? All and nothing! All, because our pedagogy is based on imitation and example. Nothing, because we don't use any form of indoctrination, and don't wish to create a hard-set picture of what each individual or child must be like.

When I meet the children, how can I be in a position where I let them be free and still give them the possibility to create forming forces and strengthen their will life so that they can meet social life with self-confidence and empathy?

It is said about children nowadays that they are very different from children of preceding generations. That might be true, but what is surely different is their surroundings. Nowadays, the children are awakened in their childhood innocence a lot earlier than before. It is not possible to judge whether that is good or bad, one can only observe it.

A Celebration of Nøkken

How do we bring childhood's gifts to the child: total acceptance, innocence, faith, trust? For me, the key has always been life in Nature, its constant changes and transformations, never the same and yet recognizable. The fact of being in Nature, and working with it with consideration and respect has been a means of bringing to present-day children (and adults) an understanding, an experience of forces that are far beyond our comprehension, but that call for our wondering. To be able to see and wonder is a driving force for life.

Regardless of where we are on the Earth, Nature is at the base of our culture and our survival. We must adjust our existence according to these natural forces: it is deeply ingrained in us. A calling for a religious force that goes beyond all religious denomination is also present in Nature. Nature's celebrations must always be an expression of the surroundings we live in. For me, the cosmic celebrations are another element. They take place at specific times all over the Earth, because they lie in a realm located far above the plain Nature form.

Let's take Easter as an example. In Denmark, Easter falls with spring. So we mix the two celebrations. We prepare a spring celebration that expresses appreciation for the arrival of spring after a very dark period. We paint (a heathen custom) and we let the Easter Rabbit hide eggs that the children must find (the hare as a fertility symbol). Then we roll those eggs down a hill so that the hardboiled eggs split in two and the yolks roll out, a symbol for the release and the ascension (Sun force) of Jesus Christ as the force of spiritual empathy. In that manner, we mix a force of Nature with a spiritual celebration. It works quite well, because we mix many old traditions with spiritual cosmic realities in a hodge-podge.

All is well because we have the seasons we have, but what happens on the other side of the earth? There it is fall, with the Lantern celebration as a Nature celebration, and Easter as a Cosmic celebration. It means that in that situation (fall on the other side of the earth), the raising of the Christ force must convey an Inner enlightenment, while in the Northern hemisphere it must be an external experience, or how else can it be?

It is incredibly exciting to deepen one's thoughts on cause and context, but that leads to considerations that are far from the main purpose of this article: to give a picture of how we practice our seasonal and cosmic celebrations so that they appear as parts of a whole instead of isolated celebrations.

I have chosen the celebrations that I feel are relevant for our kindergarten, considering the cultural background of my children and the environment they come from. I have chosen a daily rhythm that builds on a lot of outdoor experiences, because many of the children are city children with limited movement possibilities. Because we have a delightful garden and beautiful surroundings (swamps, cemetery and soccer field), although we are located only fifteen minutes by bicycle from the center of Copenhagen, it is quite natural for us to include these areas in our daily life. Every day we spend the first two morning hours outside the kindergarten: we walk twenty minutes, spend one hour at a specific place, and walk home again.

On our daily walk, we get an experience of the four elements: the whistling (or lack thereof) of the wind; the warmth of the sun, when it hides or comes out; the drumming of the rain or the splashing of the puddles; the changing states of the earth, wet, dry, planted or not, etc.

At the same time, Nature embraces us, and

A Garden for Kids

it makes a great difference where we are in the course of the year. Each time has its own quality, and each season makes us remember the previous one and look forward to the next one. Nature helps us remember prior experiences and build up joy for upcoming ones. That expresses itself quite naturally in the different phases that the children go through in the six years they spend in the kindergarten.

The seasons never start and never end: they are like a wheel that is constantly in motion. If the seasons don't lie next to one another, they reflect one another over the ones in between, but the other way around. For instance, our children always start singing Christmas songs in the late spring just before summer. They dance around spruce trees that have put forth new shoots and look just as if they had decorated themselves the way we, in Denmark, decorate them and dance around them at Christmas.

The complementary celebrations take place, to a large extent, at the same time as the real seasonal celebrations, and that is where all our pedagogical work lies. This way we carry out the celebrations so that there is a context with the whole course of the year—a weaving in and out from one to the next —and yet some kind of orderly sequence, so that the formative forces clearly shine through, because all has a meaning, nothing is indifferent.

The art is to understand Nature as a rhythmical breath, instead of a beat that ticks separate events.

A Harvest Celebration

To start with harvesting time is like going directly to the end of a good book. At harvesting time we harvest our diligence! On the outside, we harvest the crops given to us by the Earth, depending on how good we have been at observing Nature, at sowing in a timely manner and at taking care of our crops.

For me, harvesting grains is an archetypal experience. I still ask myself whether it is not a bit artificial to bring my city children to the countryside and see a farmer harvest with a scythe and gather sheaves to bring them back to the kindergarten. Nowadays children know that all this is done with huge machines and they cannot connect a scythe with a grain field (if they have seen one in the first place). I still stubbornly keep the farm visit for all families as a shared outing and a sensory experience, because I see some archetypal movements in the sweeping of the scythe through the grain and in the sound of the meeting between scythe and grain. As we stand outside in the field, we hear the wind, the sky is high above, and we can see far on every side. To have seen the farmer's genuine movements makes it also possible to make the right movements during singing games, and I think that it is very important to be able to imitate the proper movements instead of just making limp and vague movements—children need genuine actions.

After the farm visit, we use about fourteen days to "harvest". The grain stands in sheaves in the garden to be seen and touched. We sing harvest songs, and after a couple of days, we thresh the grain. All the children stand in a circle and as we sing the harvest songs, we go around the small harvest sheaves. When we get to the part of the song that says: "Do you know how the farmer threshes" we all bend down, take a sheaf and thresh the grain from the ears on the white sheet that lays in the middle. We repeat that threshing motion time after time, some children with great care, some with a lot of force, while others simply watch (the small ones are sleeping, at that time). Seeing the grain jump out of the ears is a magic trick that is commented upon with excitement. When all the bundles have been threshed, two adults grab each their end of the sheet, as the children stand a bit back to the side, and one, two, three, we throw grain and chaff in the air. The wind will blow the chaff away and the grain falls back, nice and clean, into the sheet.

To feel grain is a blissful experience. "Me too!" "Me too!"—all the children stream by and bury their hands in the heap of grain, a magical moment.

After that, the small hand-driven grain mills come out and the children take turn grinding (we have about seven mills for sixteen children). For days, they grind and grind to make flour during the afternoon hours. On our morning outings, we take along the straw, which we adults, helped or watched by the children, make into wreaths and various braided objects. We sing as we work. This is an industrious time.

Harvest work takes place all over the garden. Fruit, berries, and vegetables must be harvested—at different times, though— and they must be processed or dried, flowers must be watered, animals must be fed, and rabbits must be shorn. It is a wonderfully industrious time with lots of work to do. We round it off with a harvest celebration to which the parents, bringing homemade cakes, are invited one afternoon. We have baked bread and prepared elderflower juice from before the summer vacation so that we are reminded of the magical time from the days before summer, when all had a different color and the atmosphere was different. On the day of the celebration, we go to a special place where we churn cream into butter in jam jars and bring it back home. We then dress with festive clothes—all the children have brought special fine harvest clothes (not new or expensive, but clothes they connect with harvest time, celebration, and joy). We all get ready and admire each other under this transformation. We shed the old and renew ourselves.

In a long line, we go to the kindergarten room, which has been decorated for the occasion with harvest sheaves, rose hips, and wild flowers. It is so beautiful! We sit by a long table and today the children get to "butter" their own bread, decide themselves what they will have on their bread, and kindly ask to be handed this or that. There is abundance; many children get their fill just by looking. After that comes the harvest story. It is made out in the garden, from the fruits and vegetables the children have brought themselves the day before. One of the caregivers has prepared a story on the theme: The king invites people to a harvest celebration, because the princess wants to get married. . . The children are as quiet as mice are. After the story, it is time to play in the garden, where children can repeat the story or

A Garden for Kids

invent new ones, or simply play in peace and quiet. The adults are busy in the garden, preparing the tables for the parents' visit.

When the parents arrive, they wait in the garden by the entrance of the kindergarten (and deliver the cakes to the helpful caregivers). When all have arrived, we all go in a singing chain to the garden towards a pile of straw.

There the parents sit and weave a light wreath or some other craft. It is important that the parents have something to do. During that time, the children play around in the garden, so that the parents can catch a glimpse of children at play. After half an hour, all are invited to the tables and we sing our mealtime song. Then we eat, we chat, and we chew. All get a beautiful wreath to take home, to be hung by the entrance door or on a wall; or to be laid on a table to be decorated again with various flowers. In any case, the wreath is kept until Advent Spiral time, at which time it is brought back to be transformed into an advent wreath with spruce branches from the spiral. In that manner, harvest time and the advent spiral time mesh with one another.

Our Step into Nøkken
• TINE, MOTHER OF ROSA, AGE TWO

The first time I visited Nøkken a couple of months ago I was so pleased. Not so much because of what I saw, even though it looked great, but what really caught my attention was what I felt and sensed. There was an atmosphere of peace, care, and attentiveness that only a real garden can have. Instinctively I felt that this was a sanctuary for young, new lives.

Our daughter had been in day care, but that was with a grandmother, so a kindergarten was a bit of a step in a different direction. And I was, admittedly, a tiny bit nervous about sending the apple of our eye out into the big world, all alone. But I had experienced how she sought the company of other children and raced towards them on playgrounds and streets, boldly proclaiming: "Rosa!" (My name is Rosa. Who are you?) She was burning to get out there and be with other children. The question was whether her mum and dad were ready for it.

It settled us a bit to read the book *Nøkken: A Garden for Children* and to talk with Helle, who came to visit us at home and told us about the purpose and foundation of the kindergarten and the daily routine. The only thing that bothered us slightly was that Rosa Maria would have to give up her pacifier, because we used it frequently to comfort her in the car, before sleep and in other potential crisis situations.

It was decided that my husband should go with Rosa Maria the first days, and soon the big day arrived. Off they went with backpack, waterproof clothes, rubber boots, woolen sweater, suntan lotion, down comforter, new woolen slippers—and without pacifier (though daddy had one in his pocket). We told Rosa Maria that she was going to start in kindergarten. Of course she didn't understand what that meant, but she clearly sensed that something special was about to happen and that it concerned her.

It was a very special experience to be there during the first days in the kindergarten. Each day daddy of course had to describe in detail what they had been doing, what they had been singing, where they had been going on their daily walk, what the names of the other children were, if Rosa Maria had been well, if she had been crying. . .

The proud father had one moment of crisis, when Rosa Maria burst into tears the first day he left. He had to stand outside the gate and listen, and even though she quickly stopped crying, he came home slightly pale. But Rosa Maria seemed to be floating on the clouds, full of impressions.

The only thing was this little issue with the pacifier, which we secretly continued using at home. After a couple of weeks, Helle told us they had difficulties getting Rosa Maria to sleep and asked us if we had given up the pacifier. So the mother had to admit that we found it a bit rough to go "cold turkey" just like that. The consequence was that she was doing it every day in the kindergarten, which was actually worse.

So we braced ourselves and talked with Rosa Maria about how she was now a big girl going to kindergarten, and that she didn't need a pacifier anymore, which she seemed to accept a lot easier than expected. Already the day after she forgot the pacifier most of the time and bravely declared "Rosa, big girl," when she found one on the floor. Then came the real test, when we were going up to our summer house for the weekend, because the pacifier had been standard equipment on all car trips. And surely enough Rosa Maria wailed all the way, but mum and dad held their ground and had to find other and better ways to comfort her, which perhaps was the real challenge we had tried to avoid. It took about a week, where Rosa Maria from time to time sulked for her pacifier while we jumped around to try to divert her attention. But since then she hasn't asked for it a single time and is doing wonderfully without it.

To see a young human being take the first frail steps towards independence is a very moving journey. We can see how Rosa Maria is growing day by day, and how good it is for the family that she has some hours where she has a life of her own.

She is very inspired about the singing, and from friends with older children in Steiner/Waldorf kindergartens we are beginning to find out which songs she learns. "Fly, little butterfly" has been the big hit all summer, and Rosa Maria has taught us to shake hands and say "thank you for today," when saying goodbye.

As first-time parents, it is fantastic to experience the extraordinary commitment and dedication we have felt from Helle and the team in Nøkken from the very first moment. A special care and consideration radiates through everything, from materials to woodwork to that extra phone call after closing time to chat about how things are going.

A wise person once said that if you take care of the edges, the middle will take care of itself. When children are given the right framework and environment, it allows them to feel safe and able to explore, grow, and develop at their own natural pace. To find a kindergarten that provides such a framework is very special in this day and age. That is what we feel we have found with Nøkken. This inspired a little poem to the garden for children:

A Garden for Kids

In the garden will I wander
In the garden, peaceful and free
Will I water all the young green shoots
So that they may grow in me

In the garden will I wander
In the garden, peaceful and free
Will I sing the song of Mother Earth
So that she may sing in me

In the garden will I wander
In the garden, peaceful and free
Will I dance the dance of twinkling fairies
So that they may dance in me

In the garden will I wander
In the garden, peaceful and free
Will I meet another and come to see
That I am not alone in me

"Graduation" Speech

• THOMAS BALSTROM, FATHER OF KAROLINE, AGE 7

The following speech was held on June 13, 2003 for the parents of the big children who were to leave the kindergarten in the summer of that year, to go on at Vidar School. Thomas Balstrom lives next door to the kindergarten.

The five big children, Aron, Filip, Karoline, Johanne, and Maja, are leaving the kindergarten today, and because we are the only parents who don't have younger children left here, we would like to take the opportunity to say a few words.

Six years have gone by since the children started here and we can truly say that it feels like the time has passed very quickly. Having followed the children here has been like watching a seed become a sprout that may feel fine in its flowerpot, but as the sprout grows further and needs more nourishment, it has to be planted into a garden because it needs more space.

Nøkken has been a lovely, safe place for the children to grow up, but now they need more space because they know all its corners so very well. They need to have some more space around them; they are longing for new challenges and new contacts.

Hopefully, they will still be climbing trees and getting soil under their nails many years from now. But now, they need to get the flowerpot soil out of their heads and learn something about letters and words, numbers, music, painting, and how to behave among bigger children and adults. Some of you children may believe that if you can just spell your own names and your brothers' and sisters' and mom's and dad's, and you can count to a hundred and one and know how many coins an ice cream costs, you may be able to come far through life without any trouble. But you may soon learn some other useful things at school, a school your parents have selected for you with great care.

I think we all agree that the grown-ups in the kindergarten have been doing what they could to live up to its reputation: a kindergarten to which many willingly travel long distances to let their beloved children be looked after. When it comes to transportation, indeed, some have had it easier than others. So, I offer respect for those who have had long daily journeys.

Now, it has been described for everybody why we have chosen this particular kindergarten. Because Nøkken is a lovely and peaceful place, an oasis in our city, well supervised by a competent board, a "leader" with a very strong personality, and a very dedicated team of employees to all of whom we would like to express our gratitude today. You have done a very good job!

The children have been very well "dressed" by you—mentally and physically. Now everybody (including their parents) has certainly learned that their juniors have to wear waterproof trousers every day, even if the weather looks fine. So also in this case it has been helpful to live nearby in case you had forgotten this by mistake. But mentally the children have been well dressed by you as well. What the upbringing at home may have missed, you have made up for and completed very well.

But as I told you in the beginning of my speech, it is time to discover something brand new. It will be good for the children—but also the parents—to take this next big step: to enter the school age. It will be thrilling to enter this new world and environment, but the basic standards and pedagogy will remain the same and be based on the same foundation as here, so we're sure that you will feel yourselves welcome and safe there in the years to come.

You will be very much missed here and you will miss Nøkken very much, too. The feelings will be reciprocal. You will miss the ones that you think are small now, but who are waiting to be the older ones. They will miss you, too, as you have always been nice to them (isn't that so?). You will miss the grown-ups, and they will miss all of you, too, so therefore it's always worth remembering that all of you children will be most welcome to pay the kindergarten a visit.

On behalf of all the families to the five "big ones," we hereby express our sincere thanks and all the best for Nøkken!

Oh, it's so good to be here!
• NINA RATZ, MOTHER OF KALPITA MARIE, AGE 5

Our daughter potters about in the garden, singing, "Oh, come sweet May", while she makes cakes and steaks from a mixture of sand, soil and clay. A certain amount of water is added, just exactly enough for it to reach the right consistency of mud quality. It is springtime, the birds are singing, our neighbor is mowing the lawn. . . wonderful! Wonderful! Wonderful!

One of the first days in spring three years ago our daughter Kalpita Marie was pottering about in another garden, singing, when she started in Nøkken—a garden for children. She quickly felt at home, got into the daily routine and settled into being in the kindergarten. Her open, flighty nature began to take root. The continuous rhythm in the kindergarten and the adults' mindful awareness of themselves as role models for the children, outdoor life with lots of exercise, fresh air, close-up experience of the seasons and the experience of being part of a community. . . all of this was helping Kalpita to land and come a little bit more down to earth. Oh, it is so good to be here!

In the beginning she had difficulties feeling her own limits and the limits of the other children. For example, she would stand too close to them, which they found uncomfortable. The adults in Nøkken helped Kalpita to discover the boundary between her and others, which of course was connected with her gain-ing a greater awareness of her own body. This meant she could be together with other children without overstepping their limits.

The fact that the adults in Nøkken view each child both as an individual and as a member of the community creates a special dynamic which is rare, and in my eyes important in becoming a whole person. The special qualities of each child are viewed as a unique and important contribution for the benefit of all, which can only make a person feel welcome as they are. This way the community is the collective sum of qualities of all the children.

I experience that Kalpita has a very strong feeling of companionship with her friends, who are all the children in the kindergarten, while at the same time unfolding her own unique and special character. She experiences a very intense, deep and intimate joy from being a child in Nøkken, which we, her parents, can of course only be delighted about.

In our summerhouse, in our little red Swedish house in the forest, we read aloud for each other in the evenings. Here, Kalpita has been able to get into the world of storytelling that she experiences so intensely on a daily basis in Nøkken. Her stories, which must fall under the category of "stories out of this world," flow freely from her. One of them was about a boy who had teeth in one of his eyes. When he was hungry and had to eat, he just had to blink and then—pop—he was chewing the food. By now he is a big boy of 80 years and close to being an adult. And so it continued. . .

As parents to a child in Nøkken, we experience that the child's everyday life is being safeguarded with much respect and care. Because of this we can let go of our daughter each morning with the feeling that we leave her in very good and safe hands.

An Interview with Helle Heckmann
• ROBERTA DUCHARME, VIROQUA, WISCONSIN

The author is a Waldorf Kindergarten teacher at Pleasant Ridge Waldorf School in Viroqua, Wisconsin. She visited Helle at Nøkken while on sabbatical in August of 1999.

This past summer I was fortunate to be able to take a class on "Care Giving the Young Child: Birth to Seven Years" with Helle Heckmann, offered by the Waldorf Teacher Development Association, Early Childhood Education Program in Detroit, under the direction of Lora Valsi. Margaret Rosenthaler, an anthroposophical nurse from Ghent, also presented. This was a long-awaited opportunity for me as I had been anxious for more information on Helle's care center and kindergarten called Nøkken, ever since I heard Helle speak at High Mowing School during the North American Kindergarten conference. A mixed-age program, where the children were outdoors for most of their day, with an age range of one to two years to nearly seven, was intriguing to me. In the school where I have taught kindergarten for the last eleven years, we spend a good portion of our day outside—on our morning walk, on our hour of outdoor play, and then at the end of the day. We also are able to walk down the block to our "wooded acre," where we have just what the name describes, an acre of land, right in town, with lots of woods and bushes, an ideal place for young children to play. We have not yet offered a program for very young children, but the interest is there, and this is the direction we need to be facing. Witness the recent name change in the Kindergarten Association recently, and the beginning of "Lifeways" in East Troy, Wisconsin.

A Celebration of Nøkken

Right beside our school, Shannon Landis created a lovely Waldorf-inspired daycare for young children, called The Violet Garden, which fed our kindergarten programs until we took it under our wing as a mixed-age kindergarten. So I felt like there was a connection between Nøkken and Pleasant Ridge ever since I first heard about it, and when Helle's book came out in English that was the beginning of the adventure that I am on right now, as I type this interview from Copenhagen, Denmark, in the dining room of Helle Heckmann's house.

How did you first come to this work with the young child?

I started out as a university student in geography and as an emancipated woman. Most of the students in my field were men. Then when I became pregnant and gave birth that changed me completely. Having a child gives you a chance to change your life. Giving birth re-opened my senses. I found that I was hearing, seeing, tasting differently and I felt love streaming from me after having this child. When I went to go back to school, to finish up my Master's degree, I found out what the childcare situation was like. In Denmark, where nearly everyone works, childcare is very much needed. What I found was that a child can be in up to six or seven different childcare situations before they go to school. That is six or seven different "I's" who are deciding how the child should behave. Often there were good caretakers under bad conditions, or people who thought that "you can always do this until you get something better." My own child started out going on Monday, healthy and happy. By Tuesday she was starting to get weak. By Wednesday she was going down. And by Thursday or Friday she was sick. It took the weekend for her to recuperate and then start all over again on Monday. When I discovered the Waldorf kindergarten I found a place where there was no stress. My daughter was given plenty of time and was met as an individual. This inspired me to go for the three-year teacher training myself.

What is your philosophy behind Nøkken?

I believe that the family is the best place in the world for the young child. I want to support the family and the woman's need to go out in the world. Women have so much power and so much in our forces that we need to use it. I wanted to create a garden where the child still can have those first seven years protected. The children in my kindergarten have the same caregivers for six years. In this day and age

where there are many divorces and many blended families, with new siblings and parents, often the kindergarten is the place where things remain the same. Siblings have priority for admission so there is also that familiarity for the children. The main idea is that we look at the needs of the child during his or her day, not just the needs of the adults. Children can grow in peace, at their own pace, in the world of nature and the outdoors, in a home environment. The kindergarten is in the garden and buildings of my own home. There is a heartbeat holding the kindergarten 24 hours a day.

Nøkken is a daycare/kindergarten, but you limit the time the children are with you to six hours per day. Why is that?

I feel that parents need to spend time with their children so that they can understand them. If the child spends six hours at kindergarten he or she can spend six hours with his or her parents and twelve hours sleeping. This also gives parents time for each other and for themselves. This time limit keeps everyone happy and not stressed out. Parents have had to approach their workplaces and request that they only work six hours a day. It definitely can mean less money to live on and a different lifestyle, but here the priority is the child again, not the adults, and the parents want to be with their children. We have a long waiting list because parents appreciate that this is a good kindergarten for their children, with the same staff, the same children, clear ideas on limits and well thought out ideals. The teachers who are with the children can end their day still smiling because they are all with the children from the time they come at 8:30 until they leave at 2:30. For the teachers it is important so that they can be whole people, the same at home and at work. The work permeates their whole lives. In Denmark, we work all year, with five weeks paid vacation. We take this time in the month of July and one week at Christmas; otherwise we are working five days a week all year round.

Why is so much of your day spent outside?

City children do not get to move very much. They are transported everywhere. In Copenhagen 70% of the people ride bikes, and the children are transported behind them. Architects create spaces that don't let children take risks and move their bodies. Children need "danger" in their lives in that they need to have physical challenges. They need to be aware of space and their bodies in space. If they are overprotected when they are young, they seek out danger later in life.

In Copenhagen it rains 60% of the time. I have built up my kindergarten outdoors for the needs of the children, to move, to be outside, and to experience our country's weather. If children are dressed properly they can be outside playing in all kinds of weather. Sunlight is also important for the Danish people because in the winter months we have so little. Being outside helps the boys in particular because many of the activities that are typically done in a Waldorf kindergarten are more interesting to girls. Boys are not typically as talkative and they need physical challenges, (as do girls also). They need to carry firewood, saw wood, carve and play imaginatively with bows and arrows and swords. They need male role models who are strong and nurturing. Our boys play with swords and push baby carriages. We always try to have male and female teachers. This availability of wide, open spaces outside promotes better social interactions and created fewer social problems.

What about the work that the adults are doing while the children are playing?

How can children build up their lives? By understanding their surroundings, for instance by seeing where food comes from, how it is processed, served, eaten, cleaned up after and disposed of. This cycle is important in everything. This is the need of young children, to create a view of what is life and how do I fit in this life? For each activity there is a beginning, a process, and an end. The apples that grow in the garden are picked and made into applesauce, eaten, and any not good enough to cook are returned to the earth through the compost. The wool is sheared from the sheep on our farm, cleaned, teased, carded, and spun or felted. Each day all of the teachers are working as the children arrive and they continue their work throughout the day as the children play alongside. Their work actually starts before the children arrive in that they must prepare inwardly for their work and then go through with it outwardly. We may use vacuum cleaners at home, but for the child to see the archetypical act of sweeping it means that the adult uses a broom, with conscious movement using it. We have to strengthen ourselves to do simple things.

This is often the most difficult, to peel away the complicated. An incident happened the other day at the park when a little eighteen-month-old girl left her teacher and group and started walking towards the road. Two older girls soon ran after her to take care she did not go into the road, but, because the adults had consciously established the physical boundaries in their minds the girl stopped at the road and turned around and came back. She had never been told "no," she just knew it.

The festivals are also weaving through the day in the activities. Now we are weaving wheat stalks and stringing rose hips, picking plums and apples. We will have the plums and apples in sauce with our porridge.

This brings us to the festivals. How are they celebrated in the Kindergarten?

For days and weeks before the festival we are preparing for it in the adult activities. The songs we sing as we wait for the younger ones to catch up as we are walking, or the nature decorations and tissue paper windows that we create inside the houses are things that lead up to the actual day of the festival. Now we are preparing for Harvest festival at the end of August. The children will bring their special clothes to school that day and fruit and vegetables from the harvest. We will have a puppet play with the harvest vegetables being the characters in the story itself. Parents can come and learn how to weave wheat stalks. At the end of September we celebrate Michaelmas in the park, on the stone steps, which is quite an impressive setting. The older children will get a sword, a blue cape, a crown, and a daffodil bulb. It is quite a solemn ceremony. Back at the kindergarten the adults have created a mountain of chairs, covered by a blue silk cloth, with gorgeous flowers and candles on it. I tell a story in this room about the dragon and courage and then there are snacks in the garden. The parents are allowed to see this alone when they come. It makes a deep impression on them.

For Martinmas we paint paper and make lanterns. There is a parent evening before the festival and the parents can make their own lanterns, too. For the festival everyone meets and walks down to the park where the lantern lighter meets us with sun, moon, and star

A Garden for Kids

cookies and then we walk back with our lanterns to the kindergarten. Our Advent spiral is done outdoors right on our kindergarten spiral in the garden. The children place candles in the snow. In December it's important not to stress out parents, so the adults do the Nativity play for the children and in the kindergarten we may make stables, bake cookies or make candles.

In January the parents are given the fairy tale, "Hans and the Twelve Months," and they are asked to make a crown for their child to be one of the kings representing one of the months. In February the children act out the play for each other for the Winter Fest Carnival. For Easter parents are asked to send blown-out eggs for decorating. We use flowers and gauze, and onion peels for dye. We go to the park and find eggs and have egg rolling down the hills. If they break, out comes the sun from the egg! We also dye wool with onion peels and make simple chicks. For Whitsun we all go to the Open Museum where we ride horses, blow bubbles and fly birds made out of pine cones and feathers. And then after summer vacation we come full circle to Harvest once again.

Can you describe the rhythm of your day?

The teachers meet outside before the children arrive. The children come between 8:30 and 9:00. I greet the parents and then the children with a handshake. The other teachers are working also but as they are doing their work they greet the parents too. By 9:00 I sing to gather the children for circle and then we greet each other and the day with a few short songs and verses. I then sing to gather everyone at the gate and off we go to the park. It is a short walk up the road and through the cemetery and then we play for an hour and a half. It is a wonderful huge place with lawns and old evergreen trees with many opportunities for creative play. The gardeners are our friends and let us play here. When we walk back the littlest ones go to their little house for lunch and the older ones to the kindergarten house where they have their meal of hot cooked grains or vegetable soup and tea. After lunch the little ones sit on their potties while the teachers do fingerplays. One by one they are put down for sleep, in wool sleeping bags, outside in prams or sleeping boxes on the open porch. The older ones go for a puppet play in the other room and then back outside to the play yard to play in the sandbox, whittle sticks, or play with the dolls and carriages while the adults sit with their own work beside them. When the little ones awake everyone has a snack of bread and cheese at the picnic tables. Soon after it is time for everyone to go home. Play is the most important thing. This is how children learn about their world, nurture their imaginations and learn to socialize. Lessons and other activities are for the adult, not for the child.

What is your work with the parents?

Parents are not a special race; we are parents too. We are all humans. The four most important skills a human can develop are: Openness, Love, Integrity and Modesty. We are like a lemniscate, with our inner life and our outer life. We go into ourselves and then we go out to meet the world. We can only separate ourselves out from parents when we work as professionals, working on our self-education, as teachers/humans. Parents have their self-education in their own way. We interweave when we are working on our common interest – the children.

I am not going to tell the parents how to live. At the same time I am working on what I want to give, clarifying what I want to do. I offer what I have thought out freely to the parents so they can, out of freedom, say "yes" or "no" to what I offer. If I can offer this to parents I can also know how to say "yes" or "no" to parents when they cross my border. This is how I work in my life.

We have to make our meetings clear in the knowledge of the child. After parents have inquired about Nøkken I give them a copy of my book to read. Before I choose a child for the kindergarten I assess what kind of child the kindergarten needs. I want to create a picture of society so there needs to be a mix of all ages and peoples. When we say yes to a child and a family the family has to really say yes to us from their hearts. Then any problems with the child or the family will be looked upon as possibilities of development.

We take four children from each age group from one-and-a-half to nearly 7. (The young ones have to be able to walk and not be dependent on breastfeeding. It is all right to still be in diapers.) We rarely take children who have already been in another program. Two weeks before the child starts, one of the other teachers and I make a home visit in the evening and we ask the parents to give us a picture of the child, about the pregnancy and birth and the child's development. We want both parents' viewpoints and support.

During the year we send out a monthly newsletter and a list of what events are happening. They are notified three days before each festival. There are parent meetings for parents of each age group, and once a year parent consultations (parent-teacher conferences). I am available for phone conversations in the evenings and on Friday mornings when I do administrative work. And parents are always welcome to visit and spend the day with us if they want. We also have a shop in the basement of my house where we sell woolen underwear, silk caps, and biodynamic vegetables and other foods for families.

What about your work with colleagues?

The work with colleagues is very important. I can renew myself with them working together in a conscious spiritual way. We meet every morning before the children come for a verse and to see what is happening in each group or with individual children. Thursday nights we meet to discuss what is coming up. I also meet with other teachers from my area of the city and with the teacher training institute since I have interns working in my kindergarten, often several at a time.

Is there anything else we should understand about Nøkken and your philosophy?

The work we do is work for the future. We are making future good parents, with our attitudes and our gestures, with the mixed-age group of young ones and older ones. It is clear to me that this is working when I see an older child making the eurythmy "B" gesture around a younger child who is crying or when I see a very young child helping another one up or patting him on the head after a fall. We are helping to foster sturdy, healthy, nurturing children who will become this way as adults.

Author's note: I would like to thank Helle Heckmann and her family for welcoming me (and my teenage son) to their home, and me to her kindergarten. It was a wonderful experience that has inspired me to go home and really work on understanding the needs of the children in our community. Helle is not trying to encourage copies of what she has created in Nøkken, but rather trying to inspire others to really think about what their particular situation needs and to understand the needs of young children. I hope this interview helps others along that path.

The Power of Imagination
• HELLE HECKMANN

Little Johanne, one year old, is standing, looking at a tree for about ten minutes. She raises her hand slowly. Out comes the forefinger. She touches the tree carefully, then a bit more courageously, then with the whole hand. She is caressing the tree. Karoline (also one year old) has been watching Johanne. She walks over and strokes the tree, still looking at Johanne. Together they laugh. They run away from the tree, and return to stroke it again and again and again.

Undisturbed, they spend an hour with this experience. This is what childhood is all about: an identification with the surroundings. Letting the surroundings become a part of oneself. The unchangeable, the safe, the ever-existing. This, only living nature can give.

"Are you hungry?" The question is asked by Sarah, age three. We (including twenty-four children from one to six years old) are out on our daily walk to the graveyard. Autumn is rapidly approaching. The wind blows refreshingly. We are all dressed well: lots of woolen clothes underneath the raingear. Sarah is poking in some soil and mud. Skillfully, she picks up a lump and shapes it in her hand. She finds a leaf that fits exactly as a serving dish for the mud ball, a hint of pebbles and a feather completing the dish. "There you go", she says seriously. "Would you like a drink with it?" "Yes, please" is the answer. "Magnus, could you help me for a minute?" Magnus is busy putting leaves on a stick. "Does it have to be right now?"

"Does it have to be right now?" Sarah repeats, looking at me expectantly. "No, I can wait until I've finished eating," I answer. The children carry on with their doings, undisturbed.

The Wolf is Coming—Perhaps

"Helle, Helle, come and have a look." Asbjarn, five-and-a-half, comes running, short of breath. "We've seen some tracks—I think they are from a wolf." Immediately we run to look at the tracks. Several of the older children are on their knees studying the large tracks of some paw. They are eagerly chatting. Knowledge is communicated between the children. In the end they are silent and turn to me. What do I have to say? I now produce a wolf-tale, which is no more than it claims to be, and which does not comment on the tracks on the ground at all. The children are listening, their eyes are totally clear, their ears are pricked up, their mouths half open. Around us the wind is blowing, other children are climbing the trees or romping about, other adults are cutting wood, but we are far gone. When the story ends we return to the present. I leave their circle, and the children continue their exploration of nature.

What makes it so important that Sarah and Magnus can sit in a puddle underneath a tree in which the wind is blowing, and in deep concentration cook dinner? What do they shape when they shape the mud balls? To me it is definitely themselves—their inner organs. Mud, soil, sand, water do not have definite shapes, they have the ability to constantly change. This is exactly what the three-to-four-year-olds need: an identification with the surrounding world. Getting dirty is a sign of health.

The four elements of earth, water, air and fire are the basic elements that children are nourished by and grow from. No shaped toys—be they wood or plastic—can compete with these materials. The seriousness with which the children play, the deep concentration, speaks for itself, and shows how important this "playing" is. Nobody needs to fight about anything; there is plenty of mud for everybody.

Asbjorn's discovery shows the five-to-six-year-old's curiosity towards the surroundings. They wish to explore, to conquer the world, but at their own level. They discover something, investigate it, use it, leave it, and transform it.

The process is the most important. Imagination changes reality—reality is changed by imagination. Had I said, "it's a dog track, obviously not a wolf track," I would have spoiled the atmosphere and ruined their experience. I do not deny that it is a dog track, because I never lie. I enrich them by telling them about something that exists in the same world as they do, in the realm of imagination, on the edge of reality. Of course, the children know that it is not a wolf track, but this is not what they asked about. They see whether I am able to grasp their world, and get carried along, that I as an adult can nourish their imagination, that I can create a soul meeting with them by telling them a story, and not a long scientific explanation.

The Simple and the True

To meet the children where they are, on the child's own ground—that is the art of education. To understand that the child's play is most serious, because through playing, the child grasps life. Through playing, the child imitates the adult world. If the children do not

A Garden for Kids

have the possibility of imitating the basic functions of life through play they will have no possibility of understanding life. If Sarah does not experience her mother cooking (one of the most important actions in life), she will have difficulties copying this situation later in life. She will have no inner images of how to approach it. If Sarah is not allowed to imitate this where she is—that is, in the puddle—she will not adapt a basic sense experience of her imitation. The important action of working the inner out in an imitation of mum and dad (the surroundings) is what playing is all about.

Whatever is available serves as a toy, the simple unprocessed materials that can do anything your imagination wishes them to. The stick that is a horse is transformed into a sword and so on. The only limits are those of the imagination. The best toys are the tools used in the household or in crafts. The simple, the true. They do not fool the senses, and they have the qualities they promise the senses.

Most toys are total abundance, a way parents and grandparents can buy the child's affection when they do not have time to spend with the child, or are bought for their own sake or needs.

The abundance of the children's room must be every parent's or child's worst nightmare. *I'm bored. I've got nothing to play with even though the shelves are full to the brim.* Dust-collectors, a useless mess. Where is the love for the teddy bear, the doll, the car? The present that was given in love and did not drown in abundance is hard to find. The child does not need the toys; the toy factories need the child!

To Be the Mother of a Child in Nøkken
• ELIZABETH HEIMDORF

I was so lucky. Cecilie began in Nøkken when she was just about two years old. Today she is eleven and unfolding as wonderfully as any mother could wish. I am so grateful to Nøkken for having given the apple of my eye such a great start. But also for what Nøkken has meant for my own development as a mother and human being. Caring hands, calm eyes, the daily rhythm, out in all kinds of weather and good porridge.

You greet each other by a handshake and eye contact. Where are you? Now we are here. The handing over is easy and respectful. I only stayed in the kindergarten the first day. Look at the chickens and rabbits, then it's not so difficult for mum to leave.

Walks in all kinds of weather, first in a pram and later holding hands with a friend, or an adult.

Soft woollen underwear in all the months with no shortcuts when it comes to clothing—only the best will do. I even got rain clothes. We also eat more and more vegetarian food at home in respect of all the good things Cecilie brings home and has digested mentally and physically.

The adults in Nøkken are very conscious of their influence as role models for our children. They hang up laundry or dig and paint, something one can copy when playing. Low voices and careful contact. Grown-up people who have thought about how fairy tales can be made real today. How the peace and rhythm, the predictable and the humor, can become part of life here and now. Food for thought, and great inspiration.

Oh, to finally become six years old and get a dagger as a birthday present from the kindergarten, and to have enough care for the younger children to know how to use it responsibly. We happily and loudly joined in singing the Danish summer songs, when the carriage took us around during Whitsuntide.

The outing of the year with picnic basket, juice and blankets. Neat and innocent—we brought home our own story and something real from those days. The harvest festival with garlands on the small heads and sale of cakes, pies, swords and fairy dresses is also an experience. We bring our own produce, grandparents and friends, and proudly show them the kindergarten—never has it been as lovely. The birthday fairy tale is something very special, to get a crown and a candle and permission to take them home. Look how the birthday gown has become smaller and how I have grown since last year. The notion of having cast off one's heavenly clothes to put on one's earthly clothes and descend for one's first birthday, to one day return again to put on one's heavenly clothing, is a very powerful and good example of the fine opening the children are invited for.

Also for those of us who are adults, the spiritual human is being molded, gently and with respect. With my daughter's introduction I have been influenced too. When we as parents join the Spiral of Advent, singing with a candle in our hands, a solemn change happens in us too. Then we rise to the dignity the children depend on us to fill out. It calls for commitment to be the mother of a Nøkken-child.

Bibliography

Baldwin, Rahima. *You Are Your Child's First Teacher.* Celestial Arts, 1989.

Britz-Crecelius, Heidi. *Children at Play: Preparation for Life.* Inner Traditions, 1986.

Davy, Gudrun and Voors, Bon. *Lifeways.* Hawthorn Press, 1983.

Drake, Stanley. *The Path to Birth.* Edinburgh, Scotland: Floris, 1979.

Foster, Nancy, ed. *The Seasonal Festivals in Early Childhood.* WECAN, 2010.

Glöckler, Michaela and Goebel, Wolfgang. *A Guide to Child Health.* Floris, 2013 (fourth edition).

Heckmann, Helle. *Childhood's Garden: Shaping Everyday Life Around the Needs of Young Children.* With companion DVD *A Summer Day in Nøkken.* WECAN, 2008

Howard, Susan, ed. *The Developing Child: The First Seven Years.* WECAN, 2004.

_____. *Working with the Angels: The Young Child and the Spiritual World.* WECAN, 2004.

_____. *The Young Child in the World Today.* WECAN, 2003.

Jaffke, Freya. *Work and Play in Early Childhood.* Floris, 1996.

_____. *Toymaking with Children.* Floris, 1987.

König, Karl. *Eternal Childhood.* Camphill Press, 1994.

_____. *The First Three Years of Life.* Floris, 1984.

Lewis, Kimberly and Weber, Susan. *Creating Connections: Perspectives on Parent-and-Child Work in Waldorf Early Childhood Education.* WECCAN, 2014.

Long-Breipohl, Renate, *Under the Stars – The Foundations of Steiner Waldorf Early Childhood Education*, Hawthorn Press, 2012.

Oppenheimer, Sharifa, ed. *What Is a Waldorf Kindergarten?* SteinerBooks, 2007.

Paulsen, Eldbjørg Gjessing. *Trust and Wonder.* WECAN, 2011.

Pikler, Emmi. *Friedliches Babys - zufriedene Mütter.* Herder, 2009 (fourth edition).

Raichle, Bernadette, *Creating a Home for Body, Soul and Spirit: A New Approach to Child Care.* WECAN, 2011 (second edition).

Ris, Margaret and Atchison, Trice, eds. *A Warm and Gentle Welcome: Nurturing Children from Birth to Age Three.* WECAN, 2011.

Salter, Joan. *The Incarnating Child.* Hawthorn Press, 1987.

Smith, Patti and Schaefer, Signe. *More Lifeways.* Hawthorn Press, 1997.

Steiner, Rudolf. *The Spiritual Guidance of the Individual and Humanity.* Anthroposophic Press, 1992.

_____. *Theosophy.* Anthroposophic Press, 1994.

Strauss, Michaela. *Understanding Children's Drawings.* Rudolf Steiner Press, 2008 (revised edition).

Thomson, John, et. al. *Natural Childhood.* Fireside, 1995.

Many of the above titles are available through WECAN's online store:

store.waldorfearlychildhood.org

Further Resources

WALDORF EDUCATION

Association of Waldorf Schools of North America

Ypsilanti, MI, USA • 612-870-8310

www.whywaldorfworks.org • awsna@awsna.org

Waldorf Early Childhood Association of North America

Spring Valley, NY, USA • 845-352-1690

www.waldorfearlychildhood.org • info@waldorfearlychildhood.org

Steiner Waldorf Schools Fellowship

Stourbridge, England • +44 (0)1384 374116

www.steinerwaldorf.org • admin@steinerwaldorf.org

Steiner Education Australia

Chatswood, New South Wales, Australia • 02 9411 2579

www.steinereducation.edu.au • sea@steinereducation.edu.au

Federation of Waldorf Schools in South Africa

Bryanston, South Africa

www.waldorf.org.za

Federation of Rudolf Steiner Schools in New Zealand

Auckland, New Zealand • +64 9 817-4386

www.rudolfsteinerfederation.org.nz • steiner.federation@gmail.com

BIODYNAMIC AGRICULTURE

Biodynamic Association

Milwaukee, WI • 262-649-9212

www.biodynamics.com • info@biodynamics.com

ANTHROPOSOPHIC MEDICINE

Association for Anthroposophic Medicine and Therapies in America

www.aamta.org

Made in the USA
Middletown, DE
27 April 2024